I believe reading Grahams Hooper's book will help shift your views on what is important and will create a hunger to explore Jesus more.

Karl Faase
CEO Olive Tree Media

I warmly commend this rich little book to you, whether you are believing, doubting, sceptical or even dismissive. This book can set you on a life-changing trajectory as you form your own responses to the big questions Jesus asked.

David Jackman
Past President of the Proclamation Trust

Jesus remains one of the most overwhelming and yet underexplored people in the history of our planet. Our calendar dates are based on him. People still name their children after him. Thousands of people every year decide to love, trust, and worship him. What are they seeing in Jesus that we're not? There are so many unanswered questions.

Graham Hooper's Do you love me? and other big questions Jesus asked *allows us to get a handle on Jesus. But Hooper flips the script. He lets Jesus ask us the 'Big Questions'. These questions will help us discover our true selves and the true Jesus. I hope you enjoy the journey.*

Sam Chan
National Communicator for City Bible Forum, Sydney, Australia

Do you love me?

and other big questions Jesus asked

GRAHAM HOOPER

a. Acorn
Press

Published by Acorn Press
An imprint of Bible Society Australia
ACN 148 058 306 | Charity licence 19 000 528
GPO Box 4161
Sydney NSW 2001
Australia
www.acornpress.net.au | www.biblesociety.org.au

ISBN 978-0-647-53331-4

First published by Morning Star Publishing in 2020,
ISBN 978-0-647-53073-3

NATIONAL
LIBRARY
OF AUSTRALIA

A catalogue record for this
work is available from the
National Library of Australia

Cover and text design and layout by John Healy

A Note on Bible References and Abbreviations

This book contains several Bible references, quoting the source book, chapter and verse. I have used the New International Version (2011) throughout.

You'll notice an abbreviation and some numbers, placed in parentheses, sitting after quotes from Scripture. The abbreviation is a shortened form of title of whichever Bible book is being quoted (e.g., John = Jn, Matthew = Mt, Romans = Rom).

This is a way of indicating which book of the Bible a passage has come from, including the chapter and verse(s) quoted, so that you can find them in their context if you want to look further for yourself.

For example, John's Gospel, chapter 14, verse 6 is represented by (Jn 14:6).

Contents

Foreword

Christian faith is commonly presented as though it were a 'leap in the dark', an irrational commitment to believing hard – fingers crossed – in a wish-fulfilling fantasy that doesn't actually exist. But nothing could be further from the reality.

Beginning with the premise that Jesus wanted his hearers to think for themselves, and ending with the most personal of all Jesus' questions – 'Do you love me?' – this book explores the very heart of Jesus' life and teaching through some of his many searching questions.

Setting each question in its original context, Graham Hooper helps us to understand why the issues they raise are the most serious and important that any human being has to face. Through its progressive development of the good news about Jesus, this book stimulates us to get thinking about its objective truth and the impact Jesus' message ought to have on our lives and our contemporary culture.

In his writing, Graham shares his personal journey with us, drawing practical examples from his own and others' experience in a warm, engaging and empathetic way. He is gifted with a clear and penetrating insight into the meaning and significance of the Bible texts he examines. He writes about what he has personally proved to be real in his own life, in his family and in a successful business career carried out in several different countries and cultures. And what Graham has built his own life on is not wishful thinking, but the realisation that Jesus, who really lived and died, really rose again – and lives today to share his eternal life with all who trust him.

I warmly commend this rich little book to you, whether you are believing, doubting, sceptical or even dismissive. Don't reject what you haven't properly investigated. This book can set you on a life-changing trajectory as you form your own responses to the big questions Jesus asked.

David Jackman,
Past President of the Proclamation Trust
London, England
February 2020

Introduction

Why do we ask questions? Because we want answers. That seems to be the obvious answer to that particular question! But is it always that clear cut?

Sure, we ask questions to get information: 'What time does the train go?' 'Do you know the way to the theatre?' 'Where do you live?'– but other questions call for less simplistic responses.

Examiners ask questions designed to get us to express what we know. Barristers question witnesses in court to test the truth of their evidence. Wise counsellors ask questions to draw out the real issues behind the depression, anger or low self-esteem of their client, to uncover problems and get them dealt with.

Children like to ask big questions, often directly and frequently at difficult moments. 'What is that for?' 'What does that mean?' One of my daughters used to ask, with questionable grammar but laser-like focus, 'Why for?'

Then there are rhetorical questions. Watching the evening news on TV, we may ask no one in particular, 'Why do politicians never keep their promises?' Waiting in the rain at a bus stop, someone mutters, 'Why do these buses never run on time?' In both cases, no answer is expected! The schoolteacher who used to ask me in some frustration, 'Hooper, why are you always playing around in class?' wasn't looking for a detailed response. He didn't want an answer at all – he wanted a change in behaviour!

We use questions to challenge one another. I had a near miss in the shopping centre car park recently while reversing out. An angry driver in the car behind shouted out, 'Didn't you see me?' Did he want an answer? No, just an apology!

So, it seems we humans ask questions for a range of reasons and with a variety of motives.

And of course, we ask questions of ourselves. 'What am I doing here? Why am I doing this job?' We may even ask questions of God.

Good teachers use questions to get their students thinking and Jesus was a *great* teacher. When I first started to read the Bible seriously I was intrigued to find that he didn't just give people information and ask them to accept it and believe it. He asked questions. And when people came to him with their questions, he often answered them with more questions! That made me increasingly curious. Why did he ask them? What response did he want? What responses did he get? And, why does it matter?

You can always tell a wise person not only by the way they answer hard questions, but by the questions they ask. Jesus was exceptionally wise, and he asked a lot of questions – big questions. We find at least 130 of them in the four Gospels, the accounts of Jesus' life in the Bible.[1] He asked questions of religious leaders, of his group of followers and of the individuals who came to him for help.

He asked direct questions, expecting an answer. He asked rhetorical questions, which he went on to answer himself. He asked questions that challenged his hearers about what they really believed. Some of his questions uncovered prejudice,

---

[1] The number of questions differs depending on how you count them. Some claim the number is 173: http://rivwarehouse.com/resources/messages/underthecushions/173questionsjesusasked.pdf. Others have counted over 300, e.g., Martin Copenhaver, *Jesus Is the Question: The 307 Questions Jesus Asked and the 3 He Answered*, Google Books, 2014. Another source identifies 137, though admits the list is 'probably not exhaustive': https://mondaymorningreview.wordpress.com/2010/05/14/137questionsjesusasked/

narrow-mindedness and religious legalism. He asked questions that laid bare the inner motives of his questioners, exposing the shallowness of their understanding of the Scriptures they claimed to believe and the God they claimed to worship.

Some of his questions were very personal and went very deep. What did people really believe? What did they *really* want in life? What were they willing to commit to?

We may sometimes ask one another quite trivial questions, but Jesus' questions all had purpose and intent, and not just for his original hearers. Because of who he is (more on that later), his questions have timeless significance. They still speak to us today.

This book confronts us with fifteen of Jesus' most penetrating questions. It ends with that most personal of them all, addressed to a close friend who had let him down badly, 'Do you love me?' Each chapter deals with one question in its context and explores why Jesus asked that particular question – and what relevance it has for us.

As you read this book, why not pick up a Bible and read some of the suggested passages? I hope the words of Jesus, particularly the questions he asked, will make you think about who he is, how he lived and died, and why that matters so much.

1. Who do you say I am?

(Matthew 16:15)

What a strange question to ask anyone!

If the boss at work gathered her team together and asked that question, how would you respond? 'What sort of question is that? Is she feeling okay? Does she really want to know?'

If your best friend took you aside and asked a question like that, you might well start to worry. 'Why is he suddenly being so introspective? Where is he going with this?'

In Lewis Carol's famous story, *Alice's Adventures in Wonderland*, Alice asks: 'Who in the world am I? Ah, *that's* the great puzzle!'[1] Back in the real world, asking questions about our personal identity sounds a little strange. And asking someone else who *they* think *we* are sounds seriously weird.

So why did Jesus ask this question?

Was he going through some sort of identity crisis? No. Around two thousand years ago, Jesus, at the age of 30, began three years of teaching and healing knowing *exactly* who he was. The Gospels make that clear (e.g., Mt 3:13–17).

But most other people around Jesus didn't have a clue who he was. Even the people who followed Jesus weren't so sure. Rumours abounded. The word on the street in first-century Judea was that Jesus was a great prophet, possibly even one of *the* great prophets of Israel – perhaps even the prophet Elijah, somehow reincarnated (Mt 16:14).

Aware of the rumours about him, Jesus put this question to his closest friends, his disciples, those he had called to follow

---

1 Lewis Carroll, *Alice's Adventures in Wonderland,* illustrated by Júlia Sardà and Sir John Tenniel, Two Hoots, London, 2019, p. 18.

him and learn from him. 'But what about you?' he asked, 'Who do you say I am?' (Mt 16:15).

Why did he ask that question? Perhaps for the same reason he asked many of his questions. He wanted his followers to *think* – and to express in their own words their growing understanding of who he was and what that meant.

They had been with him on the road for at least a year by this time. They had known him tired and hungry; they had listened to his teaching; they had seen crowds flock to hear him and the religious establishment oppose him. They had watched him heal those with lifelong disability. He had done dramatic things like raise dead people to life. He had even calmed a storm on the Sea of Galilee with a mere word of command. The people had never met anyone like him. Who was this amazing man?

Who is Jesus?

My wife and I set up our first home together on the island of Mauritius in the Indian Ocean. I worked on a port development project, and we stayed for over six years. It is a beautiful country, populated with people of just about every race, colour and religion. When you drive around the island, you see temples, shrines, churches and mosques. In one ashram we visited, there was a row of statues of five of the world's religious leaders. Jesus was on the end. It was a vivid picture of the syncretistic belief that all religions are basically the same.

This view is very common in secular Western society, where Jesus is regarded as just one of many great religious leaders alongside Buddha, Moses, Mohammed and Krishna, all standing on the same level pointing us to God, all roads leading up the same mountain.

Most Muslims respect Jesus as a prophet. Hindus regard him as a holy man. But Jesus claimed to be much more, and his disciples were beginning to understand.

Peter was given the wisdom and spiritual insight to recognise that Jesus was someone far greater than any prophet. He answered Jesus' question with great conviction: 'You are the Messiah, the Son of the living God' (Mt 16:16).[2]

Later, on the night before his death, Jesus was with a group of his closest friends, who had still not quite grasped all this. Philip, one of his disciples, said to Jesus, 'Lord, show us the Father and that will be enough for us' (Jn 14:8). Philip wanted some final, 'once and for all' miraculous unveiling of the invisible God. In reply, Jesus asked him yet another question: 'Don't you know me Philip, even after I have been with you such a long time?' He went on: 'Anyone who has seen me has seen the Father' (Jn 14:9).

Jesus was making the astonishing claim to be God in human form. Why would anyone take a claim like that seriously?

Jesus simply asked Philip to *think*, to consider what he had seen with his own eyes. By this time, Jesus' disciples had travelled with him for three years. What had they seen? A man unlike any other – a unique human being with divine power. A person who always spoke the truth. A man who showed care and compassion to needy people but spoke out fearlessly against injustice and hypocrisy. They had heard the amazing wisdom and power of his teaching about God, and they had seen him perform miracles with just a word. Jesus, quite reasonably, challenged Philip not just to believe what he said, but to remember what he had seen Jesus do and 'believe on the

---

2 'Messiah' is a Hebrew title meaning 'God's anointed king'. The New Testament Greek word is *Christos*, translated 'Christ'. The Scriptures of the Jewish people (which Christians now call the Old Testament) had foretold the coming of a person who would be a prophet like Moses and a great king like David and who would also be the 'Son of God'. Peter realised that Jesus was that person.

evidence of the works themselves' (Jn. 14:11).

They had the evidence of all that Jesus had done – his actions and miracles – as the proof that the claims he had made about himself as having come from God were true.

But Jesus didn't just *tell* his disciples who he was. He asked them questions, because he wanted them to reach their own conclusions about him based on understanding and to make their life decisions on the basis of that knowledge.

A major rethink?

When Peter first realised who Jesus was, it was more than he could take in. The Messiah, the great king promised by God's prophets for hundreds of years, had finally come, but he was so different to what Peter and all his generation had imagined. They were expecting a military leader who would forcibly deliver them from Roman rule and bring in a golden era of prosperity and peace for the Jewish nation.

But Jesus was a king unlike any other. He had no army or palace, and he had no intention of establishing a political power base. He was a man of peace, not of violence. He loved people. He helped them, taught them and healed them. He came 'to save his people from their sins' (Mt 1:21), not to save them from Roman occupation.

Peter had to do a major rethink.

Later, after Jesus' death and resurrection, Peter and the other disciples spoke boldly about Jesus in the streets of Jerusalem. Peter told the huge crowd, 'be assured of this: God has made this Jesus, whom you crucified, both Lord and Messiah' (Acts 2:36). Peter urged the people to do a 180-degree turnaround. They, too, needed a major rethink about Jesus. They claimed to believe in God and to be waiting for his promised Messiah, but they had actually rejected and killed the one sent by God to rescue them! They had got it totally wrong, and Peter urged them to admit it, to change their minds and turn to God.

But this all happened some two thousand years ago. So why does it matter who Jesus is to you and me in the twenty-first century?

Jesus today

'What do you think about Jesus?' Pose that question to a group of friends in a coffee bar and you are likely to get an embarrassed silence or a quick change of subject. In our secular society, people are happy to criticise religion or faith, but are much less comfortable talking about Jesus. Even church leaders, who appear on TV and radio talk shows, seem to prefer discussing social and political issues, or the church, rather than speaking about Jesus. But without Jesus there is no Christian faith. It all centres on him. It all hinges on who he is.

In my teens and early twenties, I barely gave Jesus a thought. I didn't want anything to do with religion. To me, Jesus was a bearded man in a long white robe who appeared in stories from my childhood, or the pale, suffering figure depicted in so much religious art.

When I started to read the Bible as an adult, I began to understand that I had to rethink all my previous assumptions. I had used the name of Jesus as a swear word, but I started to discover that he was the most important figure in human history. I learnt to accept that I had got so many things wrong. I needed a 180-degree turnaround in my beliefs (or non-beliefs) about him. I began to see that Christian faith is not mindless belief in the dogma of the church. The Jesus of the Gospels asks questions and wants me to engage my brain and *think*. He doesn't ask me to take a leap of faith into a make-believe world or to believe something I know isn't true. He invites me to take his words seriously and consider the evidence of all the things he did that point to his real identity.

I came to understand the massive implications for my life (and for the world) if Jesus truly is who he claimed to be:

- We learn what God is like by looking at Jesus' life.
- Jesus speaks with authority, not just about God, but directly for God.
- His statements about the purpose and meaning of his life and death need to be taken seriously.

For me, this was not just the end of a search. It was a new beginning.

Who do you say that Jesus is? Before you answer that, read the Gospels and see for yourself what Jesus said and did.[3]

Further reading: Matthew 16:13–20 and Acts 2:36

---

[3] There are four Gospels in the New Testament, written some 30–40 years after Jesus' death, by which time the Christian message had started to spread like wildfire around the Roman Empire. They were written by four of Jesus' followers, Matthew, Mark, Luke and John. 'Gospel' simply means 'good news'.

2. Haven't you read…?
(Matthew 12:3, 5)

'You don't believe that stuff, do you?'

Those words were spoken to me by a housemate who had noticed a Bible on my bedside table. He was very surprised that a 'seemingly intelligent person' should ever want to read the Bible. When I asked him if he had ever read it himself, he admitted that he hadn't. He had dismissed it as an old religious book not worth his attention, not relevant to his life. I found it quite ironic that he had at his own bedside a crazy science fiction story about the origins of the universe!

Actually, I could understand where he was coming from. Like many others of my generation, I had dismissed the Bible as being of no importance to my life. I was in my early twenties, living in Tanzania, when I first started to read it seriously. I was living in a tent in the Selous Game Reserve, where I was working, when I received a letter from a friend. It was 36 pages long, and it told me how his life had been turned around.

'I have come to believe that Jesus Christ is the Son of God', he wrote, 'and believing that, everything else falls into place.' I was amazed. My friend had no Christian background at all. He urged me, 'If I never ask you anything again, I ask you to pick up a Bible and start to read.' It was the best advice I ever received.

I had known some of the stories since childhood, but reading the Bible for the first time as an adult, the words of Jesus, and particularly the questions he asked, gripped me. I realised that I needed to answer some of those questions. My agnosticism started to crumble away as I was confronted with someone who struck me as the most authentic human who ever lived.

I was profoundly shaken and immensely relieved at the same time. I realised that I had finally found what was true and lasting in this tired, cynical, 'post-truth' world.

Jesus' Bible

Jesus' own 'Bible' was what we call the Old Testament. He referred to it simply as 'the Scriptures', which he believed to be God's message to the world. Jesus quoted it extensively.

In his own life, he recognised and lived by the authority of the Scriptures as God's word. At the age of 30, before beginning three years of itinerant ministry – travelling round the country teaching and healing – he experienced a period of intense temptation to give up his mission and chase after power, wealth and fame instead. In the face of each of these three temptations, Jesus quoted the Scriptures as the final arbiter of how he would live: 'It is written … It is written … It is written … ' (Mt 4:6, 7, 10).

In debate with the religious leaders who opposed him, and in teaching his followers, he frequently referred them back to the Scriptures. When people came to him with questions about the law (Mt 12:3), marriage and divorce (19:4), children (21:16), the identity of the Messiah (21:42) and the nature of God (22:31), he would ask, 'Haven't you read … ?'

Why ask that rhetorical question? Surely, to get them to think, reflect and act on what he knew they had read but not fully understood. Perhaps he might ask us a different question. 'Have you *ever* read? Why dismiss the Bible without having read it?

Jesus: the key to the Bible?

Most of us like to live under the 'My Life, My Rules' banner. We don't like anyone telling us what to do. We may find the idea that an ancient book should be telling us how to live in the twenty-first century quite absurd.

But when we read the Bible with an open mind, we find it is not just some old book of religious rules and ceremonies. The Bible is actually a library of 66 books in one book. It includes prophecy, laws, history, biography, poetry, wise sayings, letters and reflections about life. But it speaks one central message about God and his plan for this world – and the central figure in this message is Jesus.

The whole Bible, not just the Gospels, tells us about Jesus. He taught that all the Old Testament Scriptures pointed forward to him. He challenged the religious teachers of his day: 'You study the Scriptures diligently because you think that in them you have eternal life. These are the very Scriptures that testify about me, yet you refuse to come to me to have life' (Jn 5:39–40).

Let's notice carefully what Jesus said. He claimed that the Scriptures testify about *him* – that the Bible is a testimony to Jesus and that its purpose is to lead us to trust in him. What an outrageously bold claim: to declare that he is personally the key to understanding the whole Bible!

Jesus' words

But that isn't all. As well as recognising the divine authority of the Old Testament and claiming that he was central to its interpretation, Jesus believed that the words he himself spoke had the same authority. He said: 'Heaven and earth will pass away, but my words will never pass away' (Mk 13:31).

This is a staggering claim! It must rank as the most amazing statement ever made. This one man, looking ahead, seeing in the future the passing away of all human endeavours, all nations, all empires and the earth itself, predicted that the words *he* spoke in the first century will never pass away.

Words are cheap. Think of the billions of words poured out every day in written form on social media, on the internet, in books, papers, reports, legal documents, poems, songs, press releases and personal letters. How long will they be remembered? I'd bet that most of these words will be forgotten within a few days. A small percentage will be remembered for a lifetime. The works of a few great writers and speakers will survive more than a hundred years. Only the words of a very few survive longer. But this first-century Galilean carpenter's son, who became an itinerant teacher and healer, claimed his words would outlast the universe itself.

It sounds like the claim of a delusional man with a big ego! And it would be, if these words had been spoken by anyone other than Jesus.

We cannot explain Jesus away; he demands our attention. From the accounts of his life, we see that he was a man unlike any other. He healed people and even brought dead people back to life. His wisdom and teaching, once heard, is seldom forgotten. His life showed the unique combination of humility and authority and a quality of selfless love and care that has inspired millions since.

Jesus' words therefore deserve to be taken seriously. In one of his famous stories (parables), he said that if we hear his words and put them into practice, we will be building our lives on solid rock. But if we hear his words and ignore them, we will be building on shifting sands and heading for trouble. We won't have a foundation that can stand the tests of life and death. When the storms come, we will easily get knocked over (Mt 7:24–29).

2. Haven't you read…?

If Jesus' words never pass away, it means that they will never be irrelevant. They will have something vital to say in every generation and in every culture. They will stand forever as a revelation of God and a communication from God, as Jesus claimed they were. It means his words speak powerfully to us today.

Jesus' claim about his own teaching, that it will last forever, may seem too far-fetched, too exclusive, too unbelievable, for us to accept and take in.

But instead of dismissing this claim out of hand, why not consider Jesus' question, 'Haven't you read … ?' Rather than asking for blind commitment, Jesus is assuming our capacity to think and engage and to read the Bible with an open mind. He seems confident that we'll find the truth we're looking for there.

So if you're curious about Jesus' claims, take some time to read the Bible for yourself. As you do, ask God to show you its truth.

A book like no other

The Bible is no ordinary book. But why have so many totalitarian regimes tried to ban or change it? It's still happening today in some countries such as North Korea. Even the institutional church burned the first English Bibles translated by William Tyndale in the sixteenth century.[1] Why does this old book generate so much opposition? Because, throughout history, the Bible has shown itself to be radical, powerful and subversive. Radical, because it cuts across so many assumptions of secular

[1] On October 27, 1526, the Bishop of London ordered the burning of copies of Tyndale's English Bible. It seems he saw the availability of the Bible to ordinary people, in a language they could understand (English rather than Latin), as a threat to the power of the established church.

culture. Powerful, because it has changed the lives of millions for good and continues to do so. Subversive in the sense that it insists there is a higher power than any government, any human leader, including any church leader. It is not to be taken lightly.

The Bible confronts us with the claim that there is ultimate truth, which has greater authority than any consensus view of socially acceptable beliefs or the decrees of any dictator. It tells us there is a God who has revealed himself to us in his creation, in the words of Scripture and in the person of Jesus. It shows us how we can know God.

'Haven't you read … ?' Jesus asked this question on a number of occasions to get his hearers to remember and recognise the authority of the Old Testament Scriptures. He regarded the Scriptures to be as necessary for our soul as food is for our body (Mt 4:4). He said that his own words would 'never pass away' and that God's Spirit would continue to speak God's words through his chosen apostles after his death and resurrection (Jn 16:12–14). The early Christians quickly came to regard the Old Testament, the Gospels, and the writing of Jesus' apostles to be all part of 'God's Word', his verbal revelation to humankind.[2]

God has spoken – in the Bible and in the person of his Son, Jesus Christ. He has something to say to us, some questions to ask us.

Further reading: Try reading Mark's Gospel, which you can read through in around an hour.

---

2 See also Acts 20:27, 2 Peter 1:12–21; 3:15–16 and 2 Timothy 3:16.

3. Suppose one of you has a hundred sheep and loses one of them. Doesn't he ... go after the lost sheep until he finds it?

(Luke 15:4)

Last week, the headline on the front page of my daily newspaper simply said 'LOST'. It headed an article about a high-profile sports coach who had become involved in illegal drugs and corrupt deals. He had lost his job, and his wife had left him. He had lost his way in life.

That same week, on the coast near where we live, a fisherman was reported lost after his boat capsized in a storm. His family alerted the police and a massive air-sea search and rescue mission was mounted. After about six hours, the helicoper pilot spotted him, still alive, and winched him out of the ocean to safety.

Jesus spoke about people being 'lost' on a few different occasions. When he did, he meant more than simply 'going off the rails' and messing up our lives, like the sports coach I read about. He meant that we are lost in relation to God our Father and in need of rescue.

Religion is often framed in terms of people searching for God. Jesus tells us it's the other way around. God is searching for us because he cares. We are lost, and he wants to bring us home. Jesus taught this great truth through asking a simple question about sheep and shepherds. He then went on to tell three stories.

Three stories: lost sheep, lost coin and lost sons

Jesus attracted the sort of people that the religious establishment didn't want to know. 'Tax collectors and sinners' used to gather around to hear him.[1] Tax collectors were regarded as corrupt traitors, collecting taxes for the occupying Roman army and extorting more than they were legally required to collect. 'Sinners' was a general term for those regarded by the religious elite as the dregs of society: flagrant law-breakers, thieves, prostitutes. Here were two groups of people who would never be invited into polite society. But Jesus had time for them, welcomed them and shared meals with them. They knew their lives were messed up, and they were drawn to Jesus because he was unlike any religious teacher they had ever met. He was honest. He loved them and accepted them. He was 'the real deal'.

But the religious leaders criticised him: 'This man welcomes sinners and eats with them' (Lk 15:2). It was meant to be a scathing put-down. How could Jesus be a 'holy man' when he was willing to associate with people like that? But they had unintentionally recognised something at the heart of what Jesus was all about, the purpose of his life on earth. He attracted people who were marginalised and 'lost'. He had time for them and showed that God cared for them. By contrast, the proud religious people revealed by their hard-hearted, self-righteous attitude that they were the ones who were really lost.

In response to this criticism, Jesus told three stories.

First, he pictured a shepherd with a flock of sheep, one of which strayed from the fold. As Jesus looked around at those listening to him, he asked: 'Suppose one of you has a hundred sheep and loses one of them. Doesn't he leave the ninety-nine

---

[1] See, for example, Mark 2:15–17.

*3. Suppose one of you has a hundred sheep and loses one of them.
Doesn't he ... go after the lost sheep until he finds it?*

in the open country and go after the lost sheep until he finds
it?' (Lk 15:4). Notice, he begins his story with a question which
immediately engages his listeners. In a poor rural community,
loss of just one sheep from the flock was a problem. 'Wouldn't
you go out and look for it?' Jesus asks. Of course they would!
Isn't it natural and reasonable to go looking for something
valuable you have lost?

I doubt that any of us like being compared to lost sheep.
It's not a flattering picture. Sheep give all the appearance of
being low-intelligence animals. Just watch a herd of sheep
being shepherded into a fold and you'll see how they behave
– bleating, climbing over each other, running in all directions
trying to get away.

It's not the way we like to think of ourselves, is it? But that's
how the Bible pictures us: 'We all, like sheep, have gone astray,
each of us has turned to our own way' (Isa 53:6).

When we insist on living without any reference to God, he
gives us the freedom to follow our own way and wander off on
our own, even to the point of allowing us to experience some
trauma and difficulty in our lives.

And yet, to the shepherd, each sheep is of great value, and
he goes looking for them. I recently listened to a drug addict
explain how he had been freed from his addiction when he
came to faith in Jesus Christ. He said: 'I was lost in a prison of
my own making, but Christ was the only one who came to get
me out.'

Next, Jesus told the story of a poor widow who had lost
one of her ten precious coins, which was all she possessed, and
didn't rest until she found it. Picture yourself losing your keys,
your smartphone or a valuable piece of jewellery, frantically
searching for it and then finding it in your coat pocket. That
feeling of joy and relief is what Jesus describes in this story.

Then came a third story about a father and his two sons.

The younger one left home with an early payout of his share of his father's wealth. He travelled, partied hard and ended up destitute. Returning back home in a desperate state, he was amazed to find that his father not only welcomed him back but had been out looking for him, longing for his return.

But the elder brother was not so welcoming. 'Why have you treated your younger son so generously?' he asked his father. A fair question! What had the son done to deserve such a great welcome?

The father's reply? 'This brother of yours was dead and is alive again; he was lost and is found' (Lk 15:32).

This unforgettable story packs a powerful message. The younger son represents all those who are visibly and obviously lost, those looked down on, judged, criticized and condemned by decent society. He had wasted all his father's money, lived a totally self-indulgent life and reached rock bottom living in a foreign country. He knew he was lost and decided to go back home.

But the elder brother, who represents the religious leaders in the story, didn't realise that he too was lost. He had stayed home, working in his father's business, but his critical spirit, unforgiving attitude and lack of love for his brother showed that he was far away from the loving heart of his father (who represents God in Jesus' story).

Each of the three stories has a similar ending. The shepherd is delighted with finding his one lost sheep. The widow celebrates with her friends when she finds the lost coin. The father is overjoyed when his son comes home.

As he told these stories, Jesus delivered the punchline, the main point that runs through all three of them: 'I tell you that in the same way there will be more rejoicing in heaven over one sinner who repents than over ninety-nine righteous persons who do not need to repent' (Lk 15:7); and 'I tell you, there is rejoicing in the presence of the angels of God over one sinner who repents' (Lk 15:10).

Jesus wanted his listeners – and us – to grasp this simple but profound truth: God seeks *us* out – and he is overjoyed when 'lost' people are found.

Later in Luke's Gospel, Jesus met Zacchaeus, one of those crooked tax collectors who were so despised. Jesus didn't lecture him about the need to change his behaviour. Just meeting Jesus had a massive impact on Zacchaeus. He stood up in public and announced that he would give half of his possessions to the poor and pay back four times the amounts he had extorted from people. Jesus saw this radical change in Zacchaeus' thinking and behaviour and knew that God was working in this man's heart. He realised that this particular 'lost sheep' had now been found and saved. So Jesus declared to the watching crowd, 'Today, salvation has come to this house' (Lk 19:9). He then went on to sum up the whole purpose of his life in these words: 'For the Son of Man came to seek and to save the lost' (Lk 19:10).

'Doesn't he ... go after the lost sheep until he finds it?'

Why did Jesus ask this question? It wasn't a lesson in sheep farming, or a nice moral tale for children. It was to help them understand what God is really like. As the people considered Jesus' question about the one lost sheep and listened to Jesus' three stories, they learned something wonderful about God. He cares enough for lost people, even those who deliberately turn their back on him, to go out looking for them. He cares enough about *just one lost person* to search for them, even when all the others are safe.

This idea of God willingly seeking out lost people with such commitment and passion was clearly a shocking one to Jesus' first listeners. It was a view of God his hearers most likely had never imagined. In first-century Jewish culture, a despised, crooked tax collector was not worth spending time with. A young, ungrateful man who squandered his family inheritance would be disowned, not sought out and welcomed home. Perhaps that's why Jesus needed to prime them with stories about lost coins and lost sheep before he got to the lost son!

Have you ever thought of God like that? Not as a remote unknowable figure, or as a hard task master or 'the man upstairs', but as a loving father and a good shepherd? Jesus told us that God sent him to this earth 'to seek and to save the lost'. That includes all of us, whether we realise it or not.

Further reading: Luke 15

4. Are you still so dull?
(Matthew 15:16)

Exposing the problem

My first car was 25 years old when I bought it. After a few weeks, I noticed that there were several bubbles on the paintwork. I prodded one with my screwdriver, which went right through the metal and out the other side!

I took the car to the body repair workshop. The next day, I got a phone call from the foreman. 'You'd better come and have a look at this before we take it much further – it's more serious than we thought.' They had applied the blow torch and exposed the rotten body work underneath. It looked like the whole car had only been held together by a few coats of paint and some body filler.

It was a life lesson, not just about rusting cars, but about how problems can be covered up. When they are not dealt with, they get more serious.

It comes naturally to most of us to try to present ourselves to others in the best possible light and to cover up, or even deny, our shortcomings. We like to promote our successes on social media, but not our failures. It may be only when we 'crash and burn' in some major life crisis that our deeper problems are exposed.

In asking the question 'Are you still so dull?' Jesus wasn't accusing his disciples of being intellectually thick. He wasn't being unnecessarily offensive. He was probing their lack of understanding. And he was confronting them with a very big problem, one common to all human beings, which they didn't fully understand and hadn't faced up to. It's a problem we may be slow to recognise, try to cover up or explain away. It's the problem the Bible calls 'sin'.

Religion, ceremony and rules

What situation led to Jesus asking this particular question? The Jewish religious leaders had challenged Jesus about why his followers had broken traditon by not following the prescribed ritual washing ceremony before they ate dinner. While that may seem like a strange and trivial matter to us, it was a big deal for the Jewish culture Jesus was a part of (and it's still a big deal for many Jewish people today). Jesus was a rabbi – a distinguished Jewish teacher – and he and his disciples should therefore have been setting a good example in such matters of ritual cleansing.

This wasn't a matter of food hygiene and healthy eating habits. The religious leaders believed that by this ritual washing they were somehow cleansing themselves from all the defilement of the world. The food they ate would then be ceremonially clean, and therefore they would be clean in the sight of God.

But Jesus showed little interest in such traditions. He was much more concerned with people's hearts – their real selves. He called for honesty. He hated religious compliance for its own sake, as it was all show and no substance. He accused the religious leaders of hypocrisy, of being like beautiful ornate cups that look great on the outside but are filthy on the inside (Mt 23:25–26).

His disciples were worried that Jesus had offended the religious leaders. (Indeed, he had!) But Jesus was not concerned. Instead he challenged his followers, 'Are you still so dull?' Didn't they understand that it isn't the food that goes into our mouths that makes us unclean in God's sight? It's what comes out of our heart. 'The things that come out of a person's mouth come from the heart, and these defile them. For out of the heart come evil thoughts – murder, adultery, sexual immorality, theft, false testimony, slander. These are what defile a person' (Mt 15:18–20a). No amount of ritual washing can clean up that mess!

Trying to cover up our deep problems with an external show of religion is a bit like trying to fix my rusted car with a new coat of paint. It doesn't work. We might think of sin as just relating to certain actions or behaviours – the bad things we do. But Jesus taught that we have a deeper problem. We sin because we are sinful by nature. The reason we say and do bad things is because there is something rotten at the core of our being. Our true self inevitably shows itself eventually, however much we try to cover up.

Sin or self-discovery?

Our culture likes to view all talk of sin as negative. It urges us to focus only on the positives. The received wisdom of popular thought tells us that despite our shortcomings and weak points, we are basically good people. We can do anything! We can solve our problems by a process of self-discovery, self-improvement and self-empowerment, by reaching inside ourselves to unlock our true potential and answer all our problems. It sounds appealing. But is it true?

If you do an internet search for 'discovering yourself', you will find a long list of sites with titles like 'How to find yourself in 15 steps' and 'Questions to learn who you are and what will make you happy'. You will also find video clips on 'Understanding your authentic self', 'The power of discovering who you really are' and 'How to know your life purpose in 5 minutes'!

Self-focused pop-psychology is a major industry. Our airport book stores, radio programs and TV talk shows are also full of this sort of self-help, self-discovery material, offering instant solutions to life's problems. But most of this well-intentioned advice has these three things in common:

1. It claims that the real answer to all our problems lies within ourselves. We have to look *inwards* to discover it.

2. Any concept of God is usually vague and undefined.

3. There is no recognition of human sinfulness as the root cause of our problems.

But when we open the Bible, we find a completely different worldview. In contrast to our secular culture, the Bible tells us:

1. The answers are *not* all within us. Indeed, we have a great capacity for self-deception (Jer 17:9).

2. God is not vague and undefined. He has made himself known to us (Ps 19:1; Jn 1:18). He made us and has intervened in human history from *outside* this world (Jn 3:16).

3. We all have a fatal flaw called sin. It is deeply embedded in our nature. It spoils everything, and only God can deal with it (Rom 3:23).

We only need to take a look around to see this ugly reality for ourselves. It's there every day in our newsfeeds: deceit, betrayal and corruption in politics and business; marriage breakdown, child abuse and domestic violence; robbery, rape and murder.

It's easy enough to see this in other people. But what about ourselves? If we are honest, don't we see that same ugly reality *within* ourselves? Don't we see our own failings, which come to the surface when we are tired, or under pressure, when we lose our cool and lash out verbally or physically at anyone in range?

Sin is universal. The heart of the human problem is the problem of the human heart, and we are all in the same boat. Human sinfulness creates pain and misery in every culture. Every child born into the world comes with an inbuilt sin bias. Parents never have to teach their children to be selfish; it comes quite naturally!

Expressed in our selfishness, sin spoils relationships. It also leaves us not feeling good about ourselves. Expressed in our addictions, sin enslaves us. Expressed in our ignorance and atheism, sin separates us from God. According to Jesus, it also makes us 'unclean'.

But as we read the Bible, we find that the bad news gets even worse. It's not just that sin spoils our lives and our relationship with God; it's that he is our judge. We all have to meet him at the end of life to give account. Without someone to intervene on our behalf, we will all stand condemned by our stubborn refusal to accept God's authority and our unwillingness and inability to obey God's commands.

Fixing the problem

So what is the answer? What can we do? Do we need to pray and fast, go on pilgrimages, attend church or take part in other religious ceremonies? Should we meditate to become more 'God conscious'? Or do we simply need to lift our game to become better people? Will these things give us inner peace? Will they connect us with God – if he is there?

Jesus asks, 'Are you so dull?' Can't we understand that we have a serious problem that not even our best efforts at religious devotion, spirituality or self-improvement will fix?

For alcoholics, the first step to recovery is to recognise and acknowledge that they have a problem that's too big for them. So it is for all of us. The first step out of denial and into reality is to acknowledge our own sinfulness to God – and to ourselves.

The Bible talks about 'confessing our sin'. We don't need a priest for that. We can tell God directly in our own words what he already knows and ask his forgiveness. It is simply being honest before God (1 Jn 1:9).

Jesus also spoke about 'repentance' (Mk 1:15). This means saying to God, 'I want to change. I want a new me – a new start. I want to centre my life on God rather than on myself.' That radical change is exactly what Jesus gives us.

Picture how you feel after a hard day of physical work in the hot sun, a tiring session at the gym or a long, exhausting journey. You don't just feel tired; you feel dirty. Then picture how you feel when you finally get home, strip off the dirty clothes and enjoy a long shower or soak in the bath. You feel great! Because you are clean and refreshed.

A friend of mine described to me how he felt when he first understood the good news of Jesus Christ with these words: 'God made me clean on the inside. No one had ever told me that would happen.'

Further reading: Psalm 51

5. Did not the Messiah have to suffer these things and then enter his glory?
(Luke 24:26)

In memory of those who made the supreme sacrifice. We find those words, or similar, engraved on memorial stones, plaques and honour boards, in civic buildings, community centres and graveyards everywhere.

In Australia, where I live, you can find war memorials like that in the centre of most towns and villages. They are usually built from stone and engraved with the names of young men and women who died in war. Each year on Anzac Day, wreaths are laid at the memorials, and communities hold dawn ceremonies to remember the dead and how much we owe our freedom to them.

It's not just war heroes that we remember in this way. We respect and value police, fire-fighters, surf life-savers and ordinary citizens who died trying to save the lives of others. Our society honours such people for the price they paid.

For 2,000 years, the universal symbol of Christianity has been a cross. It's an emblem of a cruel and painful death, a reminder of the death of one man around AD 30, a man unlike any others, who gave his life not just to save one person but to save the world.

A man born to die

When we read any of the four Gospel accounts of Jesus' life, we find that nearly half of each book focuses on his death and the events leading up to it. He was a man born to die.

Jesus had warned his friends many times what was going to happen to him.

> Jesus took the twelve aside and told them, 'We are going up to Jerusalem, and everything that is written by the prophets about the Son of Man[1] will be fulfilled. He will be delivered over to the Gentiles. They will mock him, insult him and spit on him; they will flog him and kill him. On the third day he will rise again' (Lk 18:31–33).

What a truly horrific prospect! But Jesus spoke about it as though it was the expected and predicted outcome. Naturally enough, it was too much for his followers to take in: 'The disciples did not understand any of this. Its meaning was hidden from them and they did not know what he was talking about' (Lk 18:34).

In other words, they didn't have a clue! If Jesus was the Messiah, how could God allow him to suffer and die? How could God allow his own Son to be defeated and publicly humiliated like that?

It was only after Jesus' resurrection that the disciples began to understand.

'Did not the Messiah have to suffer these things ... ?'

It was on the evening of the day of his resurrection. Jesus was speaking to two friends while walking to the village of Emmaus. As he explained how God's prophets had foretold his death, he asked them: 'Did not the Messiah have to suffer these things and then enter his glory?'(Lk 24:26).

He was getting them to reflect on all they knew had been

---

1 'Son of Man' is a term Jesus often used to describe himself. It's a term taken from the Old Testament book of the prophet Daniel, chapter 7.

predicted about his death in the Old Testament Scriptures. But why did Jesus himself say that the Messiah would '*have* to suffer'? Hundreds of books have been written to try to explain why Jesus died, but the best explanation of all is found in the Bible itself.

So, let's look back, as Jesus himself surely did in conversation with those two friends, to the words written by the prophet Isaiah. In the famous 53rd chapter, Isaiah foretells in astonishing detail the suffering and death of the coming Messiah, and its significance, over seven hundred years before Jesus was born. I have included this extract from Isaiah's book at some length, because it is so important.

He was despised and rejected by mankind,
 a man of suffering, and familiar with pain.
Like one from whom people hide their faces
 he was despised, and we held him in low esteem.

Surely he took up our pain
 and bore our suffering,
yet we considered him punished by God,
 stricken by him, and afflicted.
But he was pierced for our transgressions,
 he was crushed for our iniquities;
the punishment that brought us peace was on him,
 and by his wounds we are healed.
We all, like sheep, have gone astray,
 each of us has turned to our own way;
and the Lord has laid on him
 the iniquity of us all.

He was oppressed and afflicted,
 yet he did not open his mouth;
he was led like a lamb to the slaughter,
 and as a sheep before its shearers is silent,
 so he did not open his mouth.

By oppression and judgement he was taken away.
 Yet who of his generation protested?
For he was cut off from the land of the living;
 for the transgression of my people he was punished.
He was assigned a grave with the wicked,
 and with the rich in his death,
though he had done no violence,
 nor was any deceit in his mouth.

Yet it was the Lord's will to crush him and cause him to suffer,
 and though the Lord makes his life an offering for sin,
he will see his offspring and prolong his days,
 and the will of the Lord will prosper in his hand.
After he has suffered,
 he will see the light of life and be satisfied;
by his knowledge my righteous servant will justify many,
 and he will bear their iniquities.
Therefore I will give him a portion among the great,
 and he will divide the spoils with the strong,
because he poured out his life unto death,
 and was numbered with the transgressors.
For he bore the sin of many,
 and made intercession for the transgressors.

(Isaiah 53:3–12)

Justice or injustice?

So how does Isaiah help us answer this big question – why did the Messiah have to suffer? At first sight his words seem to raise more questions than answers.

On a human level, both Isaiah 53 and the Gospel accounts tell us that Jesus' death was a terrible injustice. Jesus was clearly innocent. The common belief was that anyone dying on a cross must have done something really bad. The Jews believed that such people were under God's curse. But in Isaiah's prophecy, the one suffering is called 'my righteous servant' (v. 11). 'He had done no violence, nor was any deceit in his mouth' (v. 9). He had done nothing wrong and did not deserve to die. Even the Roman Governor who sentenced him to death had pronounced him innocent. It all looked like a massive injustice. A completely innocent man was hounded to death by the religious elite, who hated him because he exposed their hypocrisy, and condemned by a weak, incompetent government leader.

How could God allow such a massive injustice? To add to our questions, Isaiah then reveals that God did not just *allow* it to happen, he *intended* it to happen. 'Yet it was the Lord's will to crush him …' (v. 10). The death of Jesus was not some awful mistake. It was planned by God himself.[2] Doesn't that leave us asking: 'how could that possibly be? How could a good God do such a thing?'

As if in answer to that question, Isaiah reveals three wonderful, deep truths about the death of Jesus.

For us

He died 'for us'. 'He was pierced for our transgressions, he was crushed for our iniquities' (v. 5). Jesus' death would be for our sin, not for his. As we have seen in the last two chapters, Jesus' own assessment of the human condition is that we are 'lost' like sheep, running away from God, and unfit to be in the presence of God. Worse than that, we are all guilty of breaking God's law and turning our backs on him. How could a holy, just God accept people like us into his heaven? Can he simply

2 To see how the New Testament follows this theme see for example Acts 2:22-23; and 4:27-28

compromise his own justice, forgive us and sweep all our law-breaking, rebellion and failure under the carpet? Isaiah tells us that it was 'for the transgression of my people, he was punished' (v. 8). God's justice was done. Sin was dealt with, but, in the mercy of God, it was Jesus, the Messiah, God's Son, who bore the judgement of God in our place. As Isaiah foretold: 'the Lord has laid on him the iniquity of us all' (v. 6).

Do you find that hard to accept? Offensive even – the idea that we can't deal with all our own problems and that someone else had to die for us? Don't we grow up learning how to survive and act independently and to take pride in our self sufficiency? Think back to your childhood. Your parents try to show you how to tie your shoelaces, but you say, 'No! I can do it by myself!' In our late teens and twenties, we are naturally very pleased with ourselves when we can move out of home, set up our own place and assert our independence. God has given us humans amazing capacity for invention and the ability to plan and do great things to change this world for the better. We set great store on self-reliance and the ability to think and act for ourselves.

But as we go through life we find increasingly that there are things we cannot do. When we get sick and need an operation, aren't we thankful for the trained doctors and nurses who do for us what we can't do for ourselves? As we get older, however humbling to our pride, aren't we thankful when someone says, 'I'll do it for you, I'll go up the ladder to clean the upstairs windows.' 'I'll move that big pile of bricks you can't lift with your back problems.' 'I'll drive you to the hospital.'

But at whatever stage of life, there are some things that none of us can do. We cannot extend our lives indefinitely and we cannot make peace with God. As Isaiah foretold long ago, Jesus Christ, in his death on the cross, would do for us what we could never do for ourselves.

Peace with God

He died to bring peace between us and God. 'The punishment that brought us peace was on him, and by his wounds we are healed' (v. 5). Isaiah reveals that it is through the death of the Messiah that we have 'shalom', that sense of rightness and wholeness that only God can give. Because justice has been fully satisfied, we have nothing to fear from God. Our broken relationship with God is restored. We have peace with God. John Oswalt writes:

> 'This is the true face of God – not the stern, implacable Judge dispassionately rehearsing the endless list of our crimes, and in the end grimly meeting out exactly what we deserved. No, this Maker, this God of all the earth is our Father who will go to any lengths to see that we do <u>NOT</u> get what we deserve. 'The judgement has been taken by the Judge' who can now proclaim that there is no more judgement outstanding against the accused.'[3]

Victory … not defeat

Death would not be the end for the Messiah. As Isaiah foretold, 'After he has suffered, he will see the light of life and be satisfied' (v. 11). Jesus asked, 'Did not the Messiah have to suffer *and then enter his glory*?' The crucifixion of Jesus was a day of betrayal and shame, a seemingly overwhelming defeat of good by evil. But as the Bible reveals, and as Jesus' resurrection emphatically confirmed, it was supremely a day of victory. A day of God's judgement on our sin, but a day of salvation for sinners. A day of unthinkable human injustice, but a day of the greatest act of God's justice. A day where the hatred and cruelty of human beings was on full display, but a day when the great love of God

---

3 John Oswalt, *The Book of Isaiah*, Wm. B. Eerdmans, 1998, p599

for sinful people was truly demonstrated (Rom 5:8).

Great moments in history always seem to have these two sides. As I write this, several world leaders and war veterans are gathered in northern France to remember the D-day landings of June 1944: a day of death and misery for thousands of soldiers who died, or were injured, in the fighting. A day of long-lasting sadness for their families. But it is also celebrated as a day of victory, because it marked the beginning of the end of Nazi domination of Europe.

To paraphrase Charles Dickens, it's accurate to say about the day Jesus died, 'It was the worst of days, it was the best of days.'[4]

Greater love

Was the death of Jesus, as some people have cynically suggested, an act of 'cosmic child abuse' by God? No! Jesus willingly laid down his life. As Isaiah foretold, 'he took up our pain and bore our suffering' (v. 4). He was completely at one with God his Father in doing this. Jesus said on the night before his death, 'Greater love has no one than this: to lay down one's life for one's friends' (Jn 15:13). It's the language of voluntary self-sacrifice to save others.

In explaining all this to two puzzled people on that first Easter Sunday, Jesus asked, 'Did not the Messiah *have* to suffer these things and then enter his glory?'. He then dipped into the Old Testament Scriptures, as we have tried to do, to answer his own question. As Jesus reminded his disciples that first Easter Day, '*this is what is written*: the Messiah will suffer and rise from the dead' (Lk 24:46).

---

4 'It was the best of times, it was the worst of times' are the famous opening words of Charles Dickens classic novel, *A Tale of Two Cities*, in which one man gives his life to save another.

But even when we understand that God planned the death of Jesus, and accept that Jesus willingly sacrificed his life for us, we are still left asking in amazement, 'Why?' Why did God send his Son? Why did Jesus go through with it? But it's much more personal than that. We are left asking, 'Why would he do that for *me*?'

Jesus answers all those questions in one word. Love. God sent his only Son because he loved us (Jn 3:16). Jesus laid down his life because he loved us. Jesus' death was the ultimate act of love.

Further reading: Luke 24:13–49

6. Why are you crying? Who is it you are looking for?

(John 20:15)

The end of an era

On March 23, 2015, I was in Singapore visiting my daughter. It was the day that Lee Kwan Yew died. He had led Singapore since 1959, presiding over its growth and development into a prosperous, stable society. Several generations of Singaporeans had never known another leader of their country. There was a great sense of loss and a massive outpouring of grief and respect for what he had achieved. It was the end of an era.

When my father died, I spent some precious time with my two sisters sorting out old photos and memorabilia. A man we had known and loved all our lives had gone. Our mother had died several years before. It was a shock to recognise that we were now the 'older generation' in our family. It was the end of an era for us.

Most of us have experienced losing someone we love and can probably imagine, to some extent, how Jesus' disciples must have felt after his death. But for them, it wasn't just that someone they loved had died. They had just witnessed a grave injustice in the cruel judicial murder of an innocent man. What's more, they had believed that he was God's promised Messiah. So how could God have allowed this to happen? Their hopes were shattered. They were left on their own … or so it seemed.

It must have felt like the end of an era.

Encounter in a graveyard

It's a moving experience to walk through a graveyard and read the inscriptions. Some gravestones have messages from family, some a Bible verse or line from a poem, and others just have names and dates.

Pilate, the Roman governor who sentenced Jesus to death, ordered that an inscription be nailed to his cross: 'This is Jesus, King of the Jews.' But the tomb of Jesus had no words engraved on it. For one thing, there wasn't time! Jesus' dead body had been taken down from the cross late on Friday afternoon. His tomb was a small cave, provided by a wealthy friend. His body was laid in this tomb, and a large stone was rolled across the entrance and sealed in place. It all had to be done before the beginning of the Jewish Sabbath, when no work was allowed, not even the burying of bodies.

Fast forward to early Sunday morning. John's Gospel tells us how some of the women, who had followed Jesus and experienced the trauma of watching him die, had gone to the tomb wanting to do one final thing for him: to wrap his body with spices and give him a decent burial according to their custom.

One of his disciples, Mary, was in deep distress. After the horror of the last three days, Jesus' body was now missing. The tomb was empty, the seal broken and the stone had been rolled back. She stood in the garden by the tomb, wailing with grief and distress. Where was his body? Couldn't they leave him alone even when he was dead?

Then Jesus, in his resurrected body, appeared to Mary. But she didn't recognise him. Perhaps her head was down, her eyes clouded with tears; whatever the reason, she was not expecting ever to see him again. He was dead. That much she knew. Then Jesus asked her: 'Woman, why are you crying? Who is it are you looking for?' (Jn 20:15).

John tells us her reaction. 'Thinking he was the gardener, she said, "Sir, if you have carried him away, tell me where you have put him, and I will get him." Jesus said to her, "Mary."' (Jn 20:15–16a).

And in that moment, when he addressed her by name, Mary realised it was Jesus she was talking to.

Two strange questions

Jesus asked Mary, 'Why are you crying?' A seemingly strange question – why *shouldn't* she be crying? Even Jesus wept at the graveside of someone he loved (Jn 11:35). He was human and deeply moved by the pain that death caused.

Funerals are usually sad occasions. However much we celebrate the life and remember all the good times, there are always tears and a deep sense of loss. In our human experience, death seems to play the last card. Death cruelly separates us from those we love. It ends beautiful lives and beautiful relationships and leaves us lost, lonely and empty. Death intrudes on our comfortable lives like a very unwelcome guest.

Kurt Marti, the Swiss theologian and poet, once described death as 'counter-revolutionary'. It puts an end to one person's hope and dreams of making a better world. It is the ultimate leveller and separator, a devastating intrusion into normal life. No wonder the Apostle Paul called it 'the last enemy' (1 Cor 15:26).

There was good reason for Mary to weep, just as we mourn and grieve over the death of someone we love.

Then Jesus asked another strange question. 'Who is it you are looking for?' Was this just a conversation starter? Was he passing the time of day or playing some sort of game?

No. In Luke's account of the resurrection, he tells us about some other women who, like Mary, had gone to the tomb early on Sunday morning. They were confronted with a supernatural appearance of two men in clothes that 'gleamed like lightning', who asked, 'Why do you look for the living among the dead?' (Lk 24:5). Jesus was not in the tomb where a dead person belonged. He was alive, risen from the dead. So why look for him in a graveyard?

Does all this sound unlikely? Unbelievable even? Of course, because this is way outside our normal human experience, which tells us that death is the end of life and that dead people do not rise again.

Jesus' resurrection may be hard for the twenty-first-century rational mind to believe, but take some time to read the Bible accounts. These are not made up stories. Consider the evidence for yourself.

Evidence[1]

First, Jesus really died. It was a very public death. Eye-witnesses saw him die. It was Jesus who was crucified, not a substitute (as my Muslim friends claim). A Roman centurion personally certified his death to the governor. This centurion had driven a spear into Jesus' dead body while he was still hanging on the cross to make absolutely sure. Despite what some have theorised, there is no possible way that he was resuscitated and then went around in his mutilated body, convincing people that he had somehow conquered death!

Second, Jesus' body really disappeared from the tomb. An obvious theory here is that someone stole the body and his friends spread the myth that Jesus had somehow 'risen again'. But neither his followers nor anyone else could have stolen the

---

1 For more detailed consideration of the evidence of Jesus' resurrection, I suggest Lee Strobel's *The Case for Christ*, Zondervan, Grand Rapids, 1998.

body, because the Roman governor ordered the tomb to be sealed and assigned soldiers to guard the tomb. If the authorities had moved his body, they could easily have produced it, once the rumours started that Jesus was alive, to disprove the claims once and for all. But his body was gone, with only the strips of cloth that had been wrapped around still in place in the tomb. No one ever produced a body.

Third, there are eyewitness accounts of Jesus' post-death appearances from multiple reliable sources. Could these resurrection appearances of Jesus simply be explained as hallucination? Doesn't that seem a plausible explanation? But the problem with this theory is that Jesus appeared in his resurrection body in different places, on different occasions and to different groups of people over a period of forty days (Acts 1:3). He appeared to more than 500 people in one place at one time (1 Cor 15:5–6). This was not a hallucination or a trick. Neither was this a visitation, a ghost or apparition. Jesus ate a meal with his friends (Jn 21:10–13) and he invited Thomas, who had at first been sceptical and unbelieving, to touch the visible marks in his body left by the nails and spear (Jn 20:24–29).

Experience

But it wasn't a cool intellectual appraisal of the facts that convinced Jesus' followers that he was alive. Nor was it just the eye-witness testimony of others. It was the amazing, life-changing, personal experience of meeting Jesus in his resurrected body.

After his death, Jesus' followers were bunkered down in a room with the doors locked. They were in a state of terror. Their leader had been crucified. Were they going to suffer the same fate?

But everything changed after they met Jesus.

Jesus' followers were radically different people after the resurrection. They were full of boldness and joy. They performed miracles in Jesus' name. They formed a community of believers that showed a quality of love and care between people of different cultures not seen before (Acts 2:42–47).

What's more, these witnesses to Jesus' resurrection, previously cowardly in their actions, now willingly suffered persecution and torture and even went to their death rather than deny what they had seen with their own eyes – that Jesus had been raised to life.When threatened by the authorities, they replied, 'We cannot help speaking about what we have seen and heard' (Acts 4:20). They went out on the streets of Jerusalem, fearlessly speaking about Jesus: 'You … put him to death by nailing him to the cross. But God raised him from the dead, freeing him from the agony of death, because it was impossible for death to keep its hold on him' (Acts 2:23–24). Note that word 'impossible'. Human beings and natural processes cannot defeat God. Jesus' resurrection showed that God's power is greater than all the evil in the world, greater even than death itself.

The early followers of Jesus suffered imprisonment, beatings and death, but the message spread like wildfire around the Roman Empire. The Jews tried desperately to suppress all talk of Jesus as the Messiah, but failed. The Roman authorities persecuted the newly named 'Christians' mercilessly, but still the numbers of believers grew, and the good news of Jesus' resurrection spread.

Over the course of history, various state leaders and religious authorities have tried to stamp out Christian faith. Secular atheists today confidently predict its demise. Yet belief in Jesus' resurrection is still going strong.

A new beginning

Jesus' death may have seemed like the end of an era, but his resurrection was the new beginning of all new beginnings.

God has drawn a line forever in human history. God affirmed, and confirmed, everything Jesus had said and done by raising him from the dead. As the Apostle Paul wrote, Jesus 'was appointed the Son of God in power by his resurrection from the dead' (Rom 1:4).

Over the past two thousand years, hundreds of millions of people from every continent have claimed to experience meeting the risen Jesus, not in his resurrection body, but in a spiritual encounter with him, a real-life experience of Jesus' promise to be with us always (Mt 28:20). This is not merely an experience of Jesus living on in our memories (as we sometimes feel about our loved ones who have died) or a way of saying that his teachings live on in us. No – believers claim to experience the actual presence and power of Jesus giving them a completely new start and changing their lives for good in an obvious way. Let me share the stories of two very different people to illustrate.

John lost his mother when he was five years old. He was sent away to boarding school because his father couldn't manage. He was lost, confused and angry. In his teen years, his school principal commented that 'society needs to be protected from people like John'. Looking back, John reflected, 'It wasn't that I was a bad boy, but I was a very angry boy.' When, as a young adult, he became a Christian, his life changed. He now devotes himself to helping troubled young people and giving them a second chance at life. The risen Christ had given him a new start and changed his life. That is the testimony of every true Christian.

Australian TV and movie actor Anna McGahan described her experience like this:

> When I first read the Bible ... I read it to convince myself that it wasn't true. I was so rejected and broken and this person [of Jesus] just disarmed me because it was so personal. As soon as I started to read it, I was like, "Well, this is the story I know I believe." This person sort of came out of the page and was on my side and was my friend. I felt this deep alliance from him and acceptance like, "everything that you are – the entire mess that you are – exactly as you are right now, I am with you." [2]

Those are just the stories of two people sharing their experience of the reality of Jesus Christ today. There are millions more.

'Who is it you are looking for?' When Jesus asked Mary this question on the day of his resurrection, she was looking for his dead body. It was a life changing question because it was then and there she meet Jesus, risen from the dead. She was certainly not expecting that. It was a completely new beginning for her.

Jesus' birth, death and resurrection divided human history into BC (Before Christ) and AD (Anno Domini – 'in the year of our Lord'). When we invite Jesus into our life, there is a dividing line. It's like the end of one era and the beginning of another. This wonderful change is variously described in the Bible as being 'born again', having 'eternal life' or becoming 'a new creation'.[3] It is a completely new beginning for us.

Further reading: John 20:1–18

---

2 Anna McGahan, "Anna McGahan: I follow my body's journey", *Eternity Magazine*, Issue 105, 28 August 2019.
3 See Jn 3:3; 3:16, and 2 Cor 5:17.

7. Do you see anything?
(Mark 8:23)

When I was ten years old, I discovered that I was partially colour blind. In the eyesight test at school, I was shown a book with pictures and shapes in the form of coloured dots. 'What can you see?' I was asked. I could see the dots clearly enough, but not any shapes or pictures. I still remember the feeling of rising panic that there was something wrong with my eyesight. Later, when I discovered that some 8 percent of the male population of the country I grew up in are partially colour blind, I didn't feel so bad.

Jesus asked a similar question to a man with a much more serious problem. He was totally blind, but Jesus had started to heal him.

A two-stage healing

Mark's Gospel tells us about this man who was brought to Jesus for healing by a group of friends. They had seen Jesus' healing power in action, and they longed for their friend to have his sight restored. So Mark tells us, with eye-witness attention to detail:

> He [Jesus] took the blind man by the hand and led him outside the village. When he had spat on the man's eyes and put his hands on him, Jesus asked, 'Do you see anything?' He looked up and said, 'I see people; they look like trees walking around.' Once more Jesus put his hands on the man's eyes. Then his eyes were opened, his sight was restored, and he saw everything clearly' (Mk 8:23–25).

Why the two-stage healing? Was the man's faith somehow lacking, or was his condition so particularly difficult to heal that Jesus needed two attempts to get it right?

Clearly not. On other occasions Jesus had healed blind people with just a word (see Mk 10:46–52) and had even healed a man blind from birth (John 9). As we read Mark's Gospel carefully, we see that this two-stage process – in which the man first saw partially, and then fully – has enormous significance in symbolising the progressive opening of the disciples' eyes to Jesus' true identity and the purpose of his mission in this world. It was a parable within a miracle.

This is highlighted by the two events that sit on either side of the healing in Mark's account. First, Jesus had performed a great miracle of feeding 4,000 people with just a few loaves and fishes (Mk 8:1–10). Astonishing though this was, his disciples had not yet grasped the significance of this miracle or what it told them about Jesus' identity. He asked them 'Do you still not see or understand? Are your hearts hardened? Do you have eyes but fail to see … ?" (Mk 8:17–18). Jesus linked their spiritual blindness to the hardness of their hearts towards God.

Then, after healing the blind man, Jesus asked his disciples the question we looked at in chapter 1, 'Who do you say I am?' (Mk 8:29). Peter, with God-given insight, affirmed that Jesus was indeed the promised Messiah. Yet immediately after this high point in Peter's understanding, when Jesus began to teach them about why he 'must suffer many things', Peter reacted in a strongly negative way. He had started to understand who Jesus was, but he still didn't understand why Jesus had to die (Mk 8:32). He 'saw' – but only partially. For Peter, as for the other disciples, this fuller understanding did not come until after Jesus' resurrection. It was a two-stage process.

The point of all this? Just as Jesus opened the physical eyes of this blind man, so Jesus gives sight to 'spiritually blind' people in every generation, opening our spiritual perception so we can truly see who he is and why he died.

Spiritual blindness

The Bible has a very high view of humanity. It teaches that each individual is a unique creation, beautifully made 'in the image of God' (Gen1:27), of great value to God. At the same time, it is very realistic about the damaging effects of human sin and describes its effects in very unflattering terms. As we saw in chapters 3 and 4, we are described as being like lost sheep, separated from God. In this story, we are pictured as being 'blind' to God.

While *physical* blindness is obvious, *spiritual* blindness is not. The irony of the problem is that we don't realise that we have a problem! Martin Luther, writing way back in the 15th century, with his typically confronting language, summarised the human condition like this:

> Scripture sets before us a man who is not only bound, wretched, captive, sick and dead, but who through the operation of Satan his lord, adds to his other miseries, that of blindness, so that he believes himself to be free, happy, possessed of liberty and ability, whole and alive.[1]

It's very humbling to admit that without God we are spiritually blind, unable to know God and unable to see that we need his help to understand what life is all about. Is it a sign of weakness to admit that we need help? Is Christian faith for weak-minded people who don't have the guts or intelligence to get through life without help from a being who may or may not exist? I don't believe so. To admit our need for help from our Creator is simply being honest.

It seems that God often begins the process of opening our eyes by first alerting us to our need. It may take some crisis in our life – bereavement, a relationship breakdown or job loss –

---

1 Martin Luther, *The Bondage of the Will*, James Clarke & Co., London, 1957, p. 162.

to wake us up to our real problem. But when we are desperate enough to know the truth, we will cry out to God for help.

First contact

I worked for several years in the amazingly beautiful and diverse country of Papua New Guinea. In 1983, the Australian Broadcasting Corporation screened a film called *First Contact.*[2] It documented the encounter of a group of Europeans (the Leahy brothers) with the highland people of Papua New Guinea in the 1930s. It highlighted the astonishing truth that over one million people living in the highlands region of Papua New Guinea had experienced no contact whatsoever with white-skinned people up to that point. Meanwhile, in Europe, the learned geographers of the colonial powers of the time had confidently asserted that the highlands were uninhabited. Suddenly, at that moment of first contact, each civilisation became aware of the existence of the other – of which, to that point, they had been entirely ignorant.

So when God 'opens our eyes', we start to become aware of a spiritual world of which we had previously been ignorant – perhaps one we did not even believe existed. There is the same sense of wonderment at this 'first contact'. We discover that there is a God, that he made us, that he loves us. He opens our minds and our hearts to discover for ourselves the meaning of what he has done for us in the person of Jesus Christ.

A young friend from South Africa told me (tongue in cheek) that some of the best places he had ever slept in were churches. It was his way of saying that when his parents had dragged him along to church on a Sunday morning, he found

---

2 The film was made by Robin Anderson and Bob Connolly and won ten international awards.

the whole experience boring and lifeless, not worth his time or attention. Then, one day, he realised that God was trying to get through to him. He experienced this 'first contact'. His eyes were gradually opened, and his life was progressively changed.

Like my South African friend, every Christian can say in one way or another, 'Once I was blind; now I see'.

Jesus asked one blind man, 'Do you see anything?' If you listen to Christians telling their story of how they came to faith in Jesus Christ, you are likely to hear phrases like this: 'I began to realise …', 'I started to understand …', and, 'I began to *see.*' This dawning realisation and growing conviction is the ongoing work of Jesus in our lives.

This conviction seems to have been a gradual experience for Jesus' first disciples. So, for us, coming to faith in Jesus may be a gradual experience as we read the Bible, learn from other Christians, see the change in their lives and realise that this is the real thing. Jesus is patient and teaches us – if we are willing to learn. But for others, this is a sudden experience. The most extreme example is probably the famous conversion of Saul of Tarsus on the road to Damascus (Acts 9).

Whether our experience is sudden or gradual, the point is this: it is Jesus who opens our blind eyes to understand who he is and what that means for us.

Sir James Simpson, the British scientist who discovered chloroform, the first serious medical anaesthetic, was asked late in his life what was his greatest discovery. His unexpected reply was, 'My greatest discovery was what Jesus would be for me.'

This is truly a life-changing experience for anyone. It certainly was for me.

When we are willing to ask God to help us 'see' and understand, he has promised to answer.

Further reading: John 9

8. Why do you look at the speck of sawdust in your brother's eye and pay no attention to the plank in your own eye?

(Matthew 7:3)

In 1948, Bertrand Russell, the famous British philosopher, explained what he called 'emotive conjugation': a way of using words to present ourselves in a more favourable light than others.[1] We don't have to be grammar experts to get his point. Russell gave us three examples:

- I am firm, you are obstinate, he is a pig-headed fool.
- I am righteously indignant, you are annoyed, he is making a fuss over nothing.
- I have reconsidered the matter, you have changed your mind, he has gone back on his word.

If you like playing with words, you can have some fun thinking up more of these for yourself!

They are meant to be amusing examples of our natural human tendency to judge other people by a different standard to the one by which we judge ourselves; an illustration of our capacity for self-deception, particularly regarding the quality of our own behaviour and attitudes.

A survey in Australia asked what behaviours by professing Christians most turned off non-Christians.[2] Understandably,

---

1 See 'Emotive Conjugation', Wikipedia, https://en.wikipedia.org/wiki/Emotive_conjugation.

2 'Faith and belief in Australia', McCrindle Research, 2017, online PDF,

'abuse by church institutions' came top of the list, but 41 percent identified 'hypocrisy' and 38 percent chose 'judging others' as the biggest issues.

A critical and judgemental spirit is never attractive. Of course, religious peoople don't have a monopoly on hypocrisy. There is a lot of it about! But when it has a veneer of religion attached, then the result is particularly repulsive. This is a huge turn-off and a big barrier to many people in opening their minds and hearts to Jesus Christ.

When I came to faith in Christ in my twenties in Africa, there was a lot that was obviously wrong with my life. It would have been easy for any of the other Christians I met to point out my many shortcomings and suggest how I should change my behaviour and generally sort my life out. I am very thankful that no one did that. Instead I was welcomed and accepted as I was, as a new believer in Jesus Christ. No one lectured me. No one judged me. No one took it upon themselves to tell me where I was going wrong. God had his own ways of doing that.

To this day, I am very thankful for the wisdom of those Christians. I have since met so many people who have been turned off Jesus because professing Christians have seemed to think of themselvers as better than others and therefore somehow qualified to criticise and judge them. It's the 'holier than thou' syndrome. But Jesus told us quite clearly:

'Do not judge or you too will be judged. For in the same way you judge others, you will be judged, and with the measure you use, it will be measured to you' (Mt 7:1–2).

And then he asked this rhetorical question, which he followed up with another to drive home his point:

Why do you look at the speck of sawdust in your brother's eye and pay no attention to the plank in your own eye?

---

p. 33, https://mccrindle.com.au/wp-content/uploads/2018/04/Faith-and-Belief-in-Australia-Report_McCrindle_2017.pdf.

How can you say to your brother, 'Let me take the speck out of your eye,' when all the time there is a plank in your own eye? You hypocrite, first take the plank out of your own eye, and then you will see clearly to remove the speck from your brother's eye (Mt 7:3–5).

The plank and the speck

The problem here is not the blindness to God that we considered in the last chapter; it's a defective view of our own failings. The picture Jesus paints is meant to be ridiculous – even funny. I am to imagine myself trying to extract an irritating speck of dust from my friend's eye, while having a huge plank of wood in my own eye!

Last week I had an in-depth eye examination. It was very reassuring to find that the specialist had the vision, the lights and high-tech equipment to identify any problems in my eyes. As I was lying motionless, marvelling at her skill, I tried to imagine myself probing for a minute defect in a patient's eye if there was a great blockage in my own eye. Of course, it would be impossible! My own defective vision would make me totally unqualified and incapable of doing the job.

So Jesus challenges our natural human tendency to judge and criticise others. Why do we like to point out other people's faults, either in gossiping behind their back or face to face, when our own faults are much bigger than we realise? Why do we feel qualified to judge others when our own faults and failings are so obvious to those who know us? A friend of mine was given a T-shirt by his wife with the slogan, 'Always certain – seldom right'. I think he took the point!

Some sort of 'brain fade', or loss of clear sight, happens to us when we forget how much God has given us – and how much he has *forgiven* us. We can easily get complacent and think, 'Of course God will forgive me. That's his job – and anyway, there isn't that much to forgive. I have a few faults like anyone else, but I'm basically a good person.'

We start to overestimate our own goodness and undervalue the goodness of God. Our sight gets clouded so we no longer see ourselves clearly. We become self-righteous and critical of others. We see ourselves as up on the judge's bench rather than down in the dock. We forget that the Christian church is a community of sinners who realise they need Jesus, not the religious police! We start to show the sort of hypocrisy that is so unattractive and that Jesus hated.

How can professing followers of Jesus be like that, when Jesus most certainly was not?

Honesty, not hypocrisy

Jesus was different. He was honest.

He asks us to be honest when we worship God. If you are angry with someone, or if we have given someone reason to hold a grudge against us, Jesus says, don't bother coming to worship God. First put the relationship right, and then come to worship (see Mt 5:22–25).

Perhaps there are some personal visits or phone calls we need to make to put things right with people?

Jesus also wanted honesty in our estimation of our own character. He won't allow us the luxury of thinking of ourselves as good people just because we have not done certain things, when we are at least guilty of thinking them (Mt 5:20–30).

Jesus also exposed our inconsistency when we expect God to forgive us, but we are not prepared to forgive others – when we are hypercritical and judgemental of the failings of others but choose to ignore our own, far greater, faults (Mt 18:23–35).

He wants us to concentrate on our own integrity before worrying about criticising others.

How did Jesus treat people?

There is so much to learn from Jesus here: from his questions, his teaching, his character and from the way he treated people. He had no trace of hypocrisy. He focused on caring for the people he met and was particularly kind to those who had been battered by life and those aware of their own failings. The following encounter, recorded in John's Gospel (chapter 8), is a standout.

The Pharisees and teachers of the law in Jesus' day saw themselves as the moral guardians of the Jewish society, superior to the general population. They brought to Jesus a woman who had been caught in the act of adultery, which – according to the strict letter of the law – deserved death by stoning, as in some Islamic societies today. They asked Jesus what should be done with her, trying to trap him.

Jesus said nothing, but instead bent down and started writing with his finger in the sand. After a while he straightened up and said these famous words, 'Let any one of you who is without sin be the first to throw a stone at her' (Jn 8:7). The people started to drift away. John notes that the older ones left first. Perhaps they were more aware of their own failings than the young.

They had come to Jesus as 'judges', intent on condemning this poor woman to a violent death. They left without throwing a stone. They came with a great plank in their eyes, but they left with a clearer view of themselves and a greater understanding of Jesus.

This is Jesus at work: a man of strength and gentleness, of purity and compassion, of wisdom and insight.

He asks a question to get us to think about our attitude to other people and to challenge the way we see ourselves, 'Why do you look at the speck of sawdust in your brother's eye and pay no attention to the plank in your own eye?' (Mt 7:3).

How do we respond to that? Perhaps by asking ourselves some questions:

- How critical am I of other people?
- Are there particular faults that I love to criticise?
- How aware am I of my own faults?
- Do I need Jesus to open my eyes to the state of my life?

Further reading: John 8:1–11

9. Were not all ten cleansed? Where are the other nine?

(Luke 17:17)

Would you say that you are a thankful person? You may find that difficult to answer because people express gratitude in different ways. Some people gush with thanks for the smallest gift. Others may just smile, nod or even grunt! I guess it depends on our culture, our personality and how we are feeling at the time. Of course, it also depends on the gift.

There is a perfunctory 'thank you', when someone makes way for you in the street or allows you to go ahead of them in the checkout queue at the supermarket. You might just nod and say 'Thanks'.

Then there is a polite 'thank you'. One of my relatives used to send me a gaudy home-made patterned tie for Christmas every year. I didn't much like the ties, but I always wrote to thank her because I appreciated the time and trouble she had taken. I learnt from my parents that expressions of gratitude oil the wheels of interpersonal relationships!

But then there is a heartfelt 'thank you' when we really mean it. Picture yourself arriving home exhausted after a very difficult day to find that your flatmate has dinner ready waiting for you. Or imagine missing the last bus home, it's raining heavily and a friend comes out to pick you up. Wouldn't you be really thankful?

Even deeper than that is a 'Words can't express … ' sense of thankfulness. That's when we are so overwhelmed with what someone has done for us – looking after children when we're in hospital, making meals when we are sick – that we are almost in tears and struggling for words. A friend of mine, who had received a significant gift of money from a relative when he needed it most, wrote in a note of thanks, 'Words can't express what that gift meant to me.'

When was the last time you were profoundly thankful? When was the last time words could not express your gratitude?

Ten lepers

Luke's Gospel tells of a man whose life was touched by Jesus and who was deeply thankful (Lk 17:11–19).

In Jesus' day, people with leprosy were outcasts from society. They were made to live outside the towns and villages. When people came near, the lepers were required by Jewish law to call out a warning that they were ceremonially 'unclean' so that no one came into contact with them.

There was no known cure for leprosy at the time, so these people were excluded from normal human life and relationships. They had no hope of life improving. But Jesus was unafraid to come near them; he even touched them. Better still, he healed them.

On one occasion, Jesus came across ten lepers in a village on the border of Galilee and Samaria. Keeping their distance, they called out to him for help. On this occasion, he didn't touch them. He simply told them to go and show themselves to the priest, who in that culture also served as a sort of district health officer. The local priest was authorised to certify their 'cleansing' and readmittance to society. All ten believed Jesus' promise and did as he directed. As they went on their way to visit the priest, they were healed.

One of the ten, when he saw he was healed, came back to see Jesus, praising God 'in a loud voice', and fell down at Jesus' feet. Luke, the Gospel writer, delights to tell us that he was a

Samaritan, a foreigner, a despised enemy of the Jews at that time.

Jesus, in some amazement, asked these three questions: 'Were not all ten cleansed? Where are the other nine? Has no one returned to give praise to God except this foreigner?' (Lk 17:17–18).

I find that remarkable. These lepers had just had their whole lives changed – not just physically, but socially. They were now able to return to their work and families and be welcomed and accepted. They must have realised that they had experienced a miracle. Yet only one of the ten of those healed felt sufficiently indebted to Jesus to go back and say 'thank you'!

I wonder if that ten percent figure is indicative. Is it that only ten percent of us ever give thanks to God for anything at all? Or is it that of all the good things God does for us, we only thank him for ten percent?

Even if we profess no Christian faith or religious belief, many of us find ourselves asking God for help in a crisis. But answers to such prayers can be quickly forgotten or 'explained away' as good luck, serendipity or 'just the way things turned out'.

We are not told why nine of the ten lepers didn't go back. Perhaps in the sheer excitement of this healing miracle, they forgot. Perhaps they were busy celebrating with friends and family, or maybe they just wanted to get on with life and not look back.

Or was it that they didn't want to be associated too closely with Jesus, who was increasingly drawing opposition from the religious leaders in the community?

Whatever the reason, these nine never came close to Jesus. They benefited from his healing power but seemed to have no desire to connect with him personally.

Yet one did turn back. He was clearly driven by more than

good manners or mere politeness. To him there was something even more important than getting back to normal life. He was deeply grateful to Jesus.

It was a personal thing. He was a Samaritan leper and therefore an outsider on two counts. But he had been helped, accepted, healed and affirmed by Jesus, in whom he saw the power and goodness of God at work. He fell at Jesus' feet and praised God. He wanted to connect with Jesus who had healed him and transformed his life. That led to Jesus promising him 'wholeness', of being 'right with God' – something even deeper and longer-lasting than his healing from leprosy.[1]

Being thankful is a great contrast to the human default position of grumbling, complaining and criticising that we looked at in the last chapter. It's a very attractive alternative to the culture of entitlement that characterises Western secular society.

Thankfulness to God is a sure sign that God is at work in our lives. It springs from understanding what God has done for us and in us.

Thanksgiving

Every year, on the last Thursday of November, Americans celebrate 'Thanksgiving'. It's a celebration going back to 1621, when the Pilgrim Fathers, fleeing from religious persecution in Europe, first landed in America. It was winter. They had no food, and many of the new arrivals died of cold and disease. Some native Americans helped them with food and other gifts. Later, when the new immigrants reaped their first harvest, they made a point of thanking God for freedom, for the help they had received and for the food they now had. They

[1] All ten were 'cleansed' (healed of leprosy), but only the one who came back was promised that his faith had made him 'whole'.

were thankful to the indigenous people of the land for their kindness. They were thankful to God, and they were thankful for what God had given them. Thanksgiving was made into an annual holiday by President Lincoln in 1863.

Every year, my wife and I get invited to a Thanksgiving party. Our hosts are not Americans, nor do they profess any Christian faith, but they pause once a year to be thankful for all the good things in life that they enjoy and that most of us take for granted.

Why is it that most of us forget to be thankful for so much of the time? When Jesus asked these rhetorical questions about the lepers he had healed, he was clearly amazed at the scale of human ingratitude to the goodness of God: 'Were not all ten cleansed? Where are the other nine? Has no one returned to give praise to God except this foreigner?'

When we realise how much God has given us and how much God has done for us through Jesus Christ, we will surely want to thank him – not just once a year, but every day. We will want to affirm our connection to Jesus every day as we read the Bible and talk to him in prayer.

A friend of mine told how he has learnt to recover from dark times, when life looks particularly hard. He takes his dog for a walk, and as he walks he intentionally brings to mind all that he has to thank God for. We don't need a dog to do that, of course, but making a habit of expressing gratitude can help it sink in. I have learned from my friend that the process of taking time out to deliberately remind myself of the goodness of God is a great antidote to self-pity and gloom.

The Bible is full of 'thank you' prayers. You may like to read one of them, such as Psalm 103. Or you could try listing all the things you are thankful for and using that as your own prayer to God.

Further reading: Luke 17:11–19 and Psalm 103

10. Can any one of you by worrying add a single hour to your life?

(Matthew 6:27)

'What keeps you awake at night?'

If I ask you that question, I am not enquiring about the traffic noise outside your home, or the boisterous neighbours, or whether you have sick children. Rather, I am asking what concerns you about your work or your family. What is front of mind for you in your situation? What dominates your thinking?

It's a fair question to ask anyone entrusted with responsibility – parent, supervisor, trustee, business owner or employee. If you have any responsibility for anyone or anything you are likely to find yourself worrying. Did I remember to lock the door at work? How will I deal with telling ten people tomorrow they will lose their job? How will they cope? Will my diabetic daughter remember to take her insulin?

If you lie awake worrying about your children or grandchildren, partner, friend or ageing parent, it's most likely because you care very much about them. This sort of worry is part of being human. We worry because we care.

After all, we rarely entrust people who don't care with responsibility for anyone or anything. Good managers and supervisors, and good parents, have to be 'worriers' and 'risk managers' by default. They see possible problems and make plans to mitigate those risks as far as they can. Do the brakes on my wife's car need fixing? Can my ageing father continue to manage on his own? How will my teenage daughter get safely home from the party tonight – should I go and pick her up?

There is a fine line here, though. On one side is this positive 'caring worry' that begets responsiblity, and on the other side is anxiety and fear. I suspect many of us spend much of our lives on the wrong side of that line in a state of perpetual anxiety.

This surely is what Jesus' question about worry is all about.

No worries?

'Hakuna matata … ' It's the Kiswahili phrase made famous in the musical, *The Lion King*. It means 'no worries'. It's also one of the great Australian sayings!

It's always easier to tell someone to stop worrying than it is to stop oneself. Let me confess to having spent many a sleepless night beset by worry. Lying awake at 3 am, even little problems start to take on massive proportions. A Swedish proverb tells us that 'worry makes a small thing cast a long shadow'.

How much we worry can depend on our health, our mood, our body chemistry, our personality, our ability to cope at the time. *What* we worry about is also unique to us. There is never a shortage of personal issues to consume our thoughts and demand our attention: health problems, family, money, work, friendships, the future, the environment, fear of what others think about us… and that's just for a start!

But *why* do we worry?

As we have already recognised, we worry because we care. But there are a whole range of other factors involved here.

We worry because we live in a broken world. The 24-hour newsfeeds remind us of this continually. Last evening, as I watched the TV news, I found myself analysing what messages it was conveying. There were three stories about violent attacks on innocent people, several pictures of death and mayhem on the roads, features about the worsening economy, the spread of disease and coverage of various wars and threats to peace and stability around the world. It all seemed designed to induce fear and anxiety in the viewer.

We worry also because God has given us an imagination! With our human capacity to imagine the future and think about the what-ifs, we can readily picture how things can go badly wrong. Because of this, we can easily get things out of proportion. We forget about God and get wrapped up in ourselves. We see even little things as big problems.

Worrying our lives away

A 108-year-old man was given the task of carrying the Olympic torch in the relay before the 2000 Sydney games. He was asked the secret of living so long. He replied, 'I've had a lot of worries in my life, but I've never worried about any of them.' Perhaps he got the balance right!

One survey estimated that we spend five years of our life worrying.[1] Jesus' question 'Can any one of you by worrying add a single hour to your life?' cuts to the heart of a very common human condition. Worry certainly can't lengthen our lives. But it often shortens them through anxiety-induced stress.

Jacques Ellul, the late French philosopher and sociologist, touched on this timeless problem back in the 1980s when he wrote these words:

> I don't know whether humans are and of themselves, creatures of anxiety and have been since the beginning, but I do know that today, here and now in the western world and spreading to all other cultures, anxiety holds in its clutches those who have the least reason to feel anxious. And the more happiness increases, it seems, the more people are full of dread and call themselves unhappy. The more security they have, the more they fear the morrow,

---

[1] Benenden Health, 2013

are apprehensive of the slightest violence, and live in a state of permanent precariousness. The more they consume the more they tremble at the thought of want. The easier their work gets, the more they complain of deadly tedium. The more reasons they have to play and enjoy themselves, the more they get bored and go off in search of some inexpressible novelty. The more they know, the more they discover a forbiddingly unknown universe. Everything threatens and overwhelms them … they are unhappy and living a life of inarticulate anxiety.[2]

This sort of anxiety can also prevent us from hearing what God has to say to us. It stops God's word taking root and growing in our lives, just as thorns and weeds choke a young plant. As Jesus said in his famous story of the sower: 'the worries of this life and the deceitfulness of wealth choke the word, making it unfruitful' (Mt 13:22). Worry and lack of trust prevent us from enjoying God's best for our lives.

Jesus asked, 'Can any one of you by worrying add a single hour to your life?' Answer: No!

It has been wisely noted that worry is the interest we pay on trouble *before* it comes. It's 'money' we don't really need to spend.

Worry vs. trust

Most of us feel better able to cope when we share our worries with someone who knows and understands us. We were not meant to battle through life on our own. If you have friends and family to share your worries … thank God! If we feel lonely and isolated, we can at least talk to a counsellor on one

---

2 Jacques Ellul, *Living Faith: Belief and doubt in a perilous world*, Harper and Row, New York, 1983, pp. 3–4.

of the helplines.[3]

But Jesus tells us that, best of all, we have a God who understands us and listens to us when we talk to him. We are invited to share our worries with him in prayer.

Jesus also invites us to *think*. If God created the birds, flowers and the food we eat, can't he be trusted to provide for us? Jesus asks five questions about worry (Mt 6:25–34), which he links together like this:

- 'Is not life more than food and the body more than clothes?' (v. 25)
- 'Are you not much more valuable than [the birds]?' (v. 26)
- 'Can anyone of you by worrying add a single hour to your life?' (v. 27)
- 'And why do you worry about clothes?' (v. 28)
- 'Will he not much more clothe you – you of little faith?' (v. 30)

In asking these rhetorical questions, Jesus indirectly gives us five reasons why we don't need to worry:

- God feeds the birds and cares about us more than the birds. (v. 26)
- We can't extend our life by worrying! (v. 27)
- God makes even the flowers of the fields beautiful, so he will certainly clothe us. (vv. 28–30)
- Our heavenly Father knows what we need to live. (v. 32)
- Each day has enough trouble of its own, so don't worry about tomorrow because we don't know what it will bring! (v. 34)

Jesus concludes:

So do not worry, saying, 'What shall we eat?' or 'What

---

3 E.g., Lifeline or Beyond Blue.

shall we drink?' or 'What shall we wear?' For the pagans run after all these things, and your heavenly Father knows that you need them. But seek first his kingdom and his righteousness, and all these things will be given to you as well (Mt 6:31–33).

Is Jesus saying that we shouldn't plan for the future or care about what happens tomorrow? Obviously not. We need to take responsibility for caring and planning in our family, at work and in the world. It's rather that much of our worry is unnecessary and unproductive because we have a heavenly Father.

But where do we draw this line, and how do we balance the need to *plan* with the need to *trust*? When do we simply trust God to work things out, and when do we need to act? When and how are we to rely on our own skills, experience and knowledge, and when are we to rely solely on God?

The answer from the Bible seems to be that these are the wrong questions. It is not either/or. It is both/and. For example, we may be very worried about losing our job or finding a new job. How do we handle it? If we are wise, we don't just sit around worrying ourselves sick. We pray for God's help and guidance, search opportunities on various websites, submit our resumes, make a few calls and get advice and help from friends. We pray, we plan, we act – and we trust in God. Sometimes God does provide for us in a surprising way, sometimes he guides us very clearly, but always he calls us to trust him. Jesus taught us that God is our heavenly Father who can be trusted.

Sometimes the Christian faith is made out to seem difficult and complicated. Our thinking gets confused; we lose sight of the simple and obvious and become bogged down in trivial issues that obscure the big picture. The core of Christianity is that we can have a relationship with God through Jesus, a relationship based on *trust.*

Some parts of the Bible may seem difficult to follow. But this teaching of Jesus is crystal clear. It's all about trust: trust in a person, not belief in a concept, a creed or a theological system.

Trust is the basis of our relationship with God, and much more so than in a human relationship, because we are trusting someone we cannot see. The Bible encourages us to trust God, to trust *in* him and in his Son, particularly in situations when that trust is tested.

Jesus talks about trusting God in the big issues of life and death (Jn 14:1), but he also spoke a lot about trusting him in the stuff of daily life – money, work and family. Trust in God is a great alternative to living in constant fear and anxiety. The Bible encourages us to trust him to guide and provide for us:

- When we have hard decisions to make (Prov 3:6)
- When we need things to live (Phil 4:19)
- In difficult circumstances (Rom 8:28–38)
- When we become anxious and forget God is there (Phil 4:6)

Jesus tells us plainly that God is good. He is a loving Father. Rather than living in anxiety, fear and doubt, we are invited to talk to our heavenly Father about our worries and trust him for the outcomes.

It is in this context of the trustworthiness of God that Jesus asks, 'Why do you worry?' We may not be able to stop worries crowding into our minds, but we can decide how to deal with them.

Further reading: Matthew 6:25–34

11. What do you want me to do for you?

(Mark 10:51)

When I was in my late 30s, I went through a period when I was not enjoying my work. I went in to see my boss to tell him. After listening for a few minutes, he stopped and simply asked, 'What do you want?'

He wasn't offering me a blank cheque to increase my pay, but he was trying to get me to explain more clearly why I was so unhappy and unsettled. It was a very wise question, and it stopped me in my tracks. I had come into the meeting grumbling about a whole range of things that were bugging me. But what was the *one thing* above all others that I wanted? The question crystallised my thinking so that I was able to tell him honestly and directly, in one sentence, what I wanted him to do about the issues on my radar. It was a landmark meeting in my working life, and I look back with gratitude to that single direct question: 'What do you want?'

A cry for help

Jesus asked a similar question. He was travelling on foot to Jerusalem when a blind man called out loudly to him for help. Jesus stopped and asked the blind man what he wanted him to do.

That must have sounded like a pointless question to a casual onlooker. Presumably, the blind man wanted food or money. In that culture, a blind person had no way of earning a living except by begging. There was no social welfare safety net, no government assistance.

But this man, named Bartimaeus, wasn't calling for material assistance. He seemed to have had some insight into who Jesus really was. He called out, 'Jesus, Son of David have mercy on me'. 'Son of David' was a kingly title. Perhaps he had heard the rumours that Jesus may be the promised Messiah. He had most probably heard stories of how Jesus had healed other blind people and had a secret hope that Jesus would do the same for him. But, he didn't express that at first. He just called out to Jesus for help. Many in the crowd told him to keep quiet, but he didn't care what they thought. He wanted Jesus to hear him.

So Jesus stopped and called him to come over. Mark describes Bartimaeus' response: 'throwing his cloak aside, he jumped to his feet and came to Jesus' (Mk 10:50). His cloak was probably his most valuable possession; it provided somewhere to collect the coins he was given and probably also served as his blanket at night. But in his haste to get to Jesus he just threw it aside.

Then Jesus asked this very direct question: 'What do you want me to do for you?'(Mk 10:51).

Jesus had great insight into people's lives, so why did he bother to ask the question? It seems he wanted Bartimaeus himself to articulate his need, to say clearly what he really wanted from Jesus.

And Bartimaeus did. He knew exactly what he wanted. It wasn't money or food. 'Rabbi, I want to see,' he answered, and Jesus restored his sight.

It wasn't the first time Jesus had asked that sort of question. One day in Jerusalem he was walking near the pool of Bethesda, where crowds of sick and disabled people used to gather. Jesus spoke to a man who had been unable to walk for 38 years. Jesus asked him: 'Do you want to get well?' (Jn 5:6). Here was another seemingly strange and unnecessary question, but it was actually a very wise and direct question, which had the desired purpose. The needy man told Jesus clearly what he wanted. He wanted to be able to walk, and Jesus healed him.

Asking God

If Jesus already knows what we need, then why do we need to ask? It's a good question, and the Bible does not give us any simple answer. But we do know that God invites us to tell him our needs and say clearly what we want him to do for us, to 'pour out [our] hearts to him' (Ps 62:8).

In your life right now, what is the one thing above others that you would like?

You may have a whole list of things that you think would solve your problems and make you happy: 'I want a job.' 'I want to find a life partner.' 'I want a baby.' 'I want better health.' 'I want a place to live.' 'I want more money.'

But if you met Jesus and he looked you in the eye and asked, 'What is it you *really* want?' your answer may well be very different. 'I want to be free from fear.' 'I want to know if God is really there.' 'I want to be sure what will happen when I die.' The real need in your life may be much deeper than you are normally prepared to admit to.

Jesus asked in these two encounters: 'What do you want me to do for you? Do you want to get well?' He taught us that it is okay to ask God for things we need and for things we long for. In the famous 'Lord's Prayer', he taught his disciples to pray every day for food, forgiveness, the grace to forgive others, and for guidance and deliverance from temptation and evil. Then he told his disciples two stories (Lk 11:5–13).

The first story is about a man who has unexpected visitors, arriving late after a long journey. They are hungry, but he has no food to give them. So he goes round to his friend's place at midnight, beats on the door and asks for three loaves of bread

(vv. 5–8). His friend's response? 'Go away, it's late, the door is locked, all the family are asleep in bed … I don't want to wake the children!' But the man won't give up. He keeps calling and knocking and eventually the tired friend gets up and gives him what he wants.

The point of the story? Even a reluctant, grumpy, neighbour will help you out because of your desperate need and persistence, however inconvenient it might be. How much more will a loving, patient God answer our prayers.

The second story is about a father-son relationship in a typical human family. Many grow up with bad father experiences, with drunken, violent, abusive or neglectful fathers, or fathers who leave and are never seen again. But here, Jesus pictures a Dad who, though flawed like all of us, at least wants to do the right thing by his children. He asks, 'Which of you fathers, if your son asks for a fish, will give him a snake instead? Or if he asks for an egg, will give him a scorpion?' (vv. 11–12).What a ridiculous scenario! Surely no one would behave like that!

Jesus then goes on to make his point: 'If you then, though you are evil, know how to give good gifts to your children, how much more will your Father in heaven give the Holy Spirit to those who ask him.' (v. 13).

Jesus uses these human illustrations of the reluctant friend and the 'evil' father to contrast the actions of ordinary people, who are flawed and reluctant to help, with God, the 'Father in Heaven'. He is good – and he delights to give us what is good.

Sandwiched between these two stories is Jesus' famous promise: 'Ask and it will be given to you; seek and you will find; knock and the door will be opened to you' (v. 9).

No good parents give their children everything they ask for, when they ask for it, but they do try to give their children what they think they most need. So Jesus invites us to tell God what we want, and then rely on him to give us what is good because he is a loving Father.

We may not get the job, the house, the child we desperately long for and pray for. But Jesus wants us to understand that God gives us what is best for us.

The greatest gift

It's very significant how Jesus ends this teaching about prayer. He promises to all who 'ask, seek and knock' that God will give them the gift of his Holy Spirit. What, or who, is the Holy Spirit? Jesus always referred to the Holy Spirit as a person. The Holy Spirit is not an inanimate power or 'life force'. Elsewhere in the Bible, the Holy Spirit is called the 'Spirit of God', the 'Spirit of Jesus', the 'Spirit of Christ' and the 'Spirit of Truth'. The Spirit makes God real in our experience and helps us understand the Bible. When Christians speak of experiencing the resurrected Jesus, it is in the person of his Spirit. To 'ask Jesus into our life' is to ask his Spirit to come and change us to be more like Jesus and to assure us about God's truth and God's love. It is the Holy Spirit who enables Christians to do things way beyond their natural ability and strength and to endure difficulty and suffering for Jesus sake.

Jesus asks, 'What do you want me to do for you?' – a question designed to stop us in our tracks and get us to think. There may be many things we want from God right now. But, according to Jesus, the one thing he most wants to give us, and that we most need, is the gift of his Spirit.

He invites us to act on his promise: 'Ask and it will be given to you; seek and you will find; knock and the door will be opened to you' (Lk 11:9).

Further reading: Luke 11:1–13

12. How is it that you don't know how to interpret this present time?

(Luke 12:56)

What would you say are the most pressing issues of 'this present time'? Climate change? Nuclear weapons? Global pandemics? Maybe you would point to all the social problems: inequality, family breakdown, drugs, child abuse and domestic violence. Perhaps you are most concerned about the long-term effects of social media, artificial intelligence and the growing threat of cyber warfare. Where is our world heading? Will we be able to adapt and survive or is it all coming to an end?

Two minutes to midnight?

Shortly after the Second World War, a group of eminent scientists in North America established the 'Doomsday Clock'.[1] It's a symbolic clock that represents a countdown to possible global catastrophe. The closer they set the clock to midnight, the closer the scientists believe the world is to disaster. It was set at seven minutes to midnight in 1947. The latest setting is two minutes to midnight due to the increasing threats of nuclear weapons and climate change.

Is this just scaremongering? Or is it a serious and realistic scenario, an urgent wake-up call to stir a complacent world to action? Whatever your view, this isn't the work of a wacky sect;

---

[1] It has been maintained since 1947 by the members of the Bulletin of the Atomic Scientists' Science and Security Board, who are in turn advised by a governing body that includes 18 Nobel Laureates.

it's a group of learned atomic scientists doing a risk assessment of the end of civilisation. They tell us we are heading in an unsustainable direction, and they have a point. There is no shortage of issues that demand out attention and our action.

But of course, they could be wrong. It may or may not be two minutes to midnight for this tired old world. We don't know. Several historical figures have famously made fools of themselves making these sorts of predictions. In comparatively recent times, William Miller predicted the end would come in 1844, Charles Russell forecast 1914 and Harold Camping, 2011.

No one knows, and Jesus warned long ago not to believe anyone who claims that they do know. But we do have a more reliable prediction: Jesus' words that the world will end when he returns (Mt 24:29–30).

According to the Bible, the single most important thing we are to understand about the times we live in is not the deteriorating environment, global power struggles, social upheaval or technological change. It is that we live in the period of time between Jesus' first coming – his death, resurrection and ascension – and his coming again to end this present age.

In one of his many confrontations with the religious leaders of his day, Jesus challenged them: 'You know how to interpret the appearance of the earth and the sky. How is it that you don't know how to interpret this present time?'(Lk 12:56).

What did Jesus mean?

Jesus knew that his coming into the world began a new era in human history. What the prophets foretold had now happened. God had come into his own world as a human being. 'The Word became flesh' (Jn 1:14). Jesus started his three years of teaching at the age of 30 with these words about the significance of his times: 'The time has come … The kingdom of God has come near. Repent and believe the good news!' (Mk 1:15).

Jesus accused the religious leaders of being blind to the fact that the Messiah was now standing among them and that this marked the beginning of a new era. They could read the signs of the weather, but they couldn't understand the significance of 'this present time'.

Jesus was born into an ordinary working family and grew up in a small village in an unfashionable part of the country, which was an outpost of the Roman Empire. The Gospels tell us of his life, death and resurrection, as well as his ascension – his final departure from this world. But Jesus also talked a lot about the future, a time when he would come back to this earth to wind up human history.

In 1942, as Japanese forces advanced across the Asia Pacific region, General MacArthur, leader of the American forces in the Pacific, had to order his troops to retreat from their positions in the Philippines. 'I shall return,' he famously promised the Philippine people. And so he did. He led the forces that liberated the Philippines from Japanese occupation in 1944.

Jesus also made a promise. He promised to return to this earth, not as a baby and not just in one location, but in a worldwide cataclysmic display of the power of God (see e.g., Luke 21 or Matthew 24). It will be the end of history and the beginning of eternity. The Bible tells us that this world will end and that God will make a new one – and Jesus' return is the key.

Some people crack jokes about it or dismiss it as a fairy story, no more believable than some weird sci-fi fantasy. But have you read Jesus' words about this? He promised. If we can trust his words on other matters, then why not this?

Hindus and Buddhists see life as a circle and history as a wheel that keeps going around and around. The view of the Bible is that human history is more like a line. It had a beginning, and it will have an end. The God who began it will end it. Jesus promised to return, and he urges us to be ready to meet him.

Being ready

As well as asking searching questions, it seems Jesus loved to tell stories (parables) to convey deep truths. Before asking his question about understanding 'this present time', he told a story about the head of a large household who had been away attending a wedding. The servants needed to be ready for when the master came back home (Lk 12:35–38).

He told another story about the boss of a business who went away and left his staff in charge. They needed to be ready for when he came back. But what if they weren't? What if those left in charge beat people up, got drunk and convinced themselves that the boss had been away so long that he wasn't ever coming back? (Lk 12:42–48). What would happen when he did finally return? It wouldn't end well!

Jesus also told of a house-owner whose home was burgled. If the owner had known what time the thief would come, he would have prevented the break-in (Lk 12:39).

The punchline of all three stories? 'You also must be ready, because the Son of Man [Jesus] will come at an hour you do not expect him' (Lk 12:40).

Be ready. But how?

Jesus pictured two people going off to court to face the magistrate (Lk 12:57–59). He urged them to sort out their dispute *before* they got to court, lest the case end badly for them. Likewise, he calls all of us to be reconciled to God *here and now*. He warns us not to wait until we die, hoping we can negotiate a deal with God then. Rather, we are to settle things 'while we are on the way' – in this life, in 'this present time'.

Jesus' words about his coming again at the end of time are like a wake-up call. We may well worry about the state of the world. Will it all end in nuclear war or some climatic catastrophe? But Jesus challenges us to recognise there is an even bigger picture. With all our knowledge about the world and its problems, Jesus asks, 'How is it that you don't know how to interpret this present time?'

The Bible urges us to wake up to the significance of the coming of Jesus to this earth, 2,000 years ago, to recognise that this world is not going to last forever and to be ready for Jesus return. It also reminds us repeatedly that that our life is not going to go on indefinitely, and we need to be ready to meet God at any time. In the light of that, it calls for our response to God's gracious invitation to be reconciled to him, through trusting in Jesus Christ, while we still have the opportunity, in 'this present time'.

In the early years of our marriage, my wife and I lived opposite a couple who had everything going for them, a beautiful home and plenty of money in their pension plan. They bought a house in the country for their retirement and had great plans for how they would use it. Sadly, the man died just one week after retirement, leaving his wife shattered and alone.

My best friend from schooldays, who was the best man at our wedding, died from colon cancer at the age of 39. He had become a Christian in his twenties and was only recently married. In the final six weeks of his life, he helped his new wife come to trust in Jesus Christ for herself. He was an inspiring example to me.

God calls us to be ready to meet him at any time. We just don't know how long we've got.

Further reading: Matthew 24 and Romans 13:11–14

13. What good is it for someone to gain the whole world yet forfeit their soul?

(Mark 8:36)

Costly decisions

Imagine finally saving enough money for a deposit to buy an apartment only to discover, a few months later, that the building has major structural problems. You have to move out. Like all the other owners in the block, you are required to stump up additional cash for the repairs, but you don't have the funds. You can't borrow to pay the repair bills, and you can't sell. The dream turns into a nightmare. Some decisions in life turn out to be costly, though we are not always aware of the cost at the time.

Of course, there are other situations where we make a decision which we know is going to be costly. For example, if we refuse to cheat or lie just to get what we want, we may suffer for it later. A work colleague who used to travel extensively in Africa described to me in graphic detail how he had been held at a border crossing for nine hours, stripped down to his underwear and harassed for refusing to pay a bribe to the guards.

Making decisions, living with their consequences and learning painful lessons from bad decisions is all part of human experience and the process of growing in maturity.

Ben had grown up in a Christian home. He found a good

job in finance, got married and was a leader in his local church. Life was good. Then his wife was diagnosed with cancer and needed constant care. He was faced with a difficult choice: to push on with his career or to take a less demanding job and so be able to look after his wife. One morning, she woke up to find he had gone. He left his wife and turned his back on his faith. His friends were in shock. They tried to work out how this could have happened. A wise friend insightfully observed: 'Throughout his whole life, Ben has had everything laid on a plate for him. He has never before had to make a decision that cost him anything.'

Jesus often confronted his listeners with decisions that would cost them in terms of money, effort or selfless care. A wealthy young man was invited to give all his money away and follow Jesus. He chose not to (Mt 19:16–22). The 'Good Samaritan' in Jesus' famous story faced a big decision: should he stop, interrupt his journey and care for the man who had been mugged and robbed by the road side, or should he just ignore him and press on with his journey? He chose to care (Lk 10:30–37).

Jesus also asked questions about the implications of our major choices: 'What good is it for someone to gain the whole world yet forfeit their soul?' (Mk 8:36).This is perhaps the most confronting question Jesus ever asked. It is one that challenges our values, lifestyle and priorities.

Profit or loss?

'He who dies with the most toys wins.' That saying is widely attributed to Malcolm Forbes, the son of the American entrepreneur who founded *Forbes* magazine. It may have been said with a hint of humour, but it sums up a widely held view: that to be successful is to be wealthy and that life is about winning and acquiring.

Jesus' teaching is diametrically opposite. He gives us a different view of what is ultimately of value. He pictures a 'profit and loss statement' at the end of a person's life. On one side of the ledger is gain: they have gained 'the whole world' – all this life has to offer in terms of money, status, and power – they seem to have it all! But on the other side of the ledger is loss. Pursuit of wealth and success has come at a great cost. This person has forfeited their soul.

What does Jesus mean? It isn't that acquiring wealth has come at the expense of marriage or family or friendships, as it often does. He isn't just describing someone who had missed out on life's best – who had not lived authentically, true to themselves. He has a longer term view. He is talking about missing out on life with God after we die. He is asking us to consider this question: what is the net profit of our life if we live only for ourselves, ignore God and ultimately lose everything?

The words Jesus spoke to his crowd of listeners immediately prior to asking this question help us understand: 'Whoever wants to be my disciple must deny themselves and take up their cross and follow me' (Mk 8:34).

Jesus had been talking about his own death, which he clearly foresaw (Mk 8:31). He then told his followers, very plainly, that following him was going to be as potentially costly for them – that they, too, would need to 'take up their cross'.

The cost of following Jesus

If we sign a contract to buy a car, take out a loan or secure an insurance policy, it's a good idea to read the fine print and understand the terms and conditions.

If you look at Jesus' promises and invitations, however, you'll find that they don't come with fine print. The conditions are made very clear right up front. Jesus told his followers on many occasions that their lives would not be easy. Indeed, they would even need to be prepared to lose their life for his sake.

But what did Jesus mean by his call for his would-be followers to 'deny themselves'? Note, he is not asking them to deny themselves *something*, as we might give up alcohol in 'Dry July' or reduce our caffeine intake for a while. Rather it is to deny *themselves*. A cross was a place of death. To 'take up our cross' is to 'die to ourselves' and to put Jesus first. What does this mean, exactly?

Over the past 2,000 years, thousands of Christians, in just about every culture, have died for their faith. Polycarp was the first recorded Christian martyr outside of the New Testament. In the arena, at the age of 86, he was offered the choice of denying his faith in Jesus Christ or being burned alive. His reply: 'Fourscore and six years have I served him, and he has never done me injury; how then can I now blaspheme my king and Saviour?'

But we don't have to look back in history to find such stories. Attacks by militant Islamic groups on Christians, and the burning of villages and churches in countries such as Nigeria, Iraq, Pakistan and Niger, are a common occurrence today. I recently met some Afghani Christians who live constantly under the threat of death because of their Christian faith. Throughout history, many of Jesus' followers have suffered simply for the 'crime' of not being prepared to give up their faith in him.

But what about those of us who have not yet been confronted with such life-defining moments? What does it look like for us to take up our cross and follow Jesus?

The Bible suggests to us that, at the very least, it will involve:
• Identifying with Jesus publicly and being unashamed to do so (Lk 9:26)

- Identifying with fellow believers (2 Tim 1:8)
- Making our faith in Jesus the first priority in all our decisions (Mt 6:33)

Each of us has to work out in practice what this means for us at home, at work, in our relationships and in our leisure time. We may or may not be confronted by government or religious authorities to make a life or death confession of faith in Jesus, and most of us doubt that we are martyr material. But I suspect that the more we put Jesus first in the seemingly small decisions of life, the easier it will be to follow Jesus in the big ones.

The Bible encourages us to believe that the quality and attractiveness of the life to come far outweighs the cost of giving up anything in this life. The apostle Paul, who suffered a great deal for his faith in Jesus, wrote: 'I consider that our present sufferings are not worth comparing with the glory that will be revealed in us' (Rom 8:18).

An appealing message?

To 'deny ourselves' is definitely not an appealing message in our culture, which constantly urges us to affirm ourselves in order to fulfil our potential and achieve our goals. A columnist at *The Times* criticised the Christian church for the off-putting content of its message, poor marketing of its product and unattractive profiling of its image. He asked,

> When is the penny going to drop with Christianity? Death, martyrdom, suffering, pain, loss, blood, these are not concepts with which any brand would want to be identified. If that's the core of your message, no wonder you've got a problem.[1]

The writer seems to miss the point. The Christian gospel,

---

1 Robert Crampton, *The Times of London*, December 14, 2009.

the good news about Jesus Christ, is not a product to be marketed, to be adapted to suit popular taste, to be packaged and presented to people in an attractive light with the right persuasive spin. According to Jesus, the gospel is God's truth. We have no right to change it or to water it down in order to make it more attractive.

Jesus was not interested in profiling his image and presenting himself in the best possible light. Luke tells us that it was when Jesus was surrounded by large crowds that he chose to emphasise the cost of following him (Lk 14:25–35). His friends must have cringed. His popularity had been surging. Why turn people off with such difficult teaching? But Jesus was totally honest. He was interested in truth, and he loved people too much to deceive them. He didn't have that craving to be liked and admired that drives so much human activity. Rather, he focused on fulfilling the mission his Father had given him and speaking the very words of God.

A crucial choice

Jesus asks, 'What good is it for someone to gain the whole world yet forfeit their soul?' (Mk 8:36). He questions our priorities, our values and lifestyle. He knows that desire for wealth, power and happiness is deeply embedded in human nature. He challenges us to think about what is ultimately of value in life and to choose what matters most.

Further reading: Mark 8:34–38

14. You do not want to leave too, do you?

(John 6:67)

Too hard

'It's all too hard!'

That phrase may come up at your workplace when you decide that a particularly difficult course of action is not worth the effort and you start looking for a simpler solution to the problem.

It's a feeling you might express when a difficult relationship turns sour. Unravelling the complex tangle of interpersonal issues, differing needs and conflicting priorities seems impossibly difficult, and you decide to break up.

Most of us have a 'too hard basket' where we leave issues unresolved, because we just don't have the mental or emotional energy to sort them out – or we don't see a solution in sight.

Jesus' disciples came to a point when following him started to look 'all too hard'. It wasn't because they were being harassed or persecuted. Rather, it was their difficulty in understanding some of Jesus' teaching, particularly when they tried fitting that in with their preconceived ideas. Many gave up and turned away.

Jesus asked those who stayed, 'You do not want to leave too, do you?' (Jn 6:67).

This situation arose after Jesus had performed the amazing miracle of feeding 5,000 people with a few loaves and fishes (Jn 6:1–15). He started to explain that he was the real 'bread of life', describing himself as the true bread 'that came down from heaven' (Jn 6:41). The religious leaders thought that this was ridiculous and started to grumble. 'Isn't this Jesus, the son of Joseph whose father and mother we know? How can he now say "I came down from heaven?"' (Jn 6:42).

Jesus went on to explain (Jn 6:43–65), but it made the situation worse when he referred to the bread being his own flesh which he gave 'for the life of the world' (v. 51). Grumbling turned to argument: 'Then the Jews began to argue sharply among themselves, 'How can this man give us his flesh to eat?' (v. 52).

Even then, Jesus didn't soften or dilute what he was saying. He repeated the same message publicly in the synagogue at the town of Capernaum: 'Whoever eats my flesh and drinks my blood has eternal life' (v. 54).

It was then that his own followers decided it was all too much: 'On hearing it, many of his disciples said, "This is a hard teaching. Who can accept it?"' (v. 60).

Was this some sort of grotesque cannibalism? What did Jesus mean? It was only later, as he celebrated the Jewish Passover meal with his disciples on the night before he died, that he made clear what he had been talking about. Matthew describes what happened like this:

> While they were eating, Jesus took bread, and when he had given thanks, he broke it and gave it to his disciples saying, 'Take and eat; this is my body.' Then he took a cup, and when he had given thanks, he gave it to them saying, 'Drink from it all of you. This is my blood of the covenant, which is poured out for many for the forgiveness of sins' (Mt 26:26–28).

This was their 'last supper' together, the precursor to the communion service that has been celebrated by Christian churches all round the world for the past 2,000 years. It is both a remembrance and a celebration. As a remembrance, it is a solemn looking back to the death of Jesus. The breaking of a loaf of bread symbolises his body that was broken in his death on a cross. The wine symbolises his blood that was shed. It is also a celebration, recognising that his death brings forgiveness for all who accept it. This is surely what Jesus meant when he talked about 'eating his flesh' and 'drinking his blood'. The bread and wine were symbols of his body and blood.

This is easier to understand with the benefit of two millennia of Christian history. But Jesus' words about 'eating his flesh' and 'drinking his blood' seemed strange and disturbing to those who first heard them, It's hardly surprising that his disciples found this very difficult to accept at the time – and that some even stopped following him.

A searching question

Why did Jesus allow this seemingly deteriorating situation to develop? It looked like a PR disaster. He'd had 5,000 people eating out of his hand (no pun intended!), only to go and upset most of the crowd, and especially the religious leaders, with this strange talk. Now he had alienated even his own disciples.

But Jesus never tried to promote his own profile. He always acted and spoke to help people understand more about God to whoever was open to receive him. So he challenged his few remaining followers with this question: 'You do not want to leave too, do you?'(Jn 6:67).

Jesus' searching question had the effect of making his closest followers get clear on where they stood. I picture Jesus looking his disciples straight in the eye as he asked this question.

A wonderful answer

Peter knew where he stood. He answered straightaway. 'Lord, to whom shall we go? You have the words of eternal life. We have come to believe and to know that you are the Holy One of God' (Jn 6:68–69).

Jesus' teaching is not always easy. His call on our life, to take up our cross and follow him, is certainly not easy. But as Peter expressed it, there really isn't anywhere else to go! Jesus is the real thing; the unique 'Holy One of God'. His words are powerful, true and life-giving.

If we turn away from Jesus, where will we go? To whom will we turn?

Perhaps you have tried following Jesus in the past but have given up. Perhaps you are close to giving up now. You may be disillusioned with the many obvious failures of Christians and Christian churches. You may have had some bad experiences where you feel God has let you down. You may find the teaching of the Bible just too hard and out of sync with popular culture. None of your friends seem interested in Jesus, so why should you be different? Could they be right after all?

So what do we do? Go back to trying to find truth and meaning only in our work, our leisure or our human relationships? All are good gifts from God, but there are no lasting answers there. It all passes away so quickly.

Do we try another religion or worldview? How could we exchange our trust in the living Son of God, who loved us and died for us, for a human system of beliefs and ceremonies? Why would we expect to find any lasting comfort there?

But Jesus' question, and Peter's response, confront us with the truth that knowing Jesus is the most important and valuable experience this world can offer. Leaving him is a path to nowhere.

'Lord, to whom shall we go? You have the words of eternal life.'

Further reading: John 6

15. Do you love me?
(John 21:16)

This is perhaps the most direct personal question one human being can ask another. There is really nowhere to hide from such a question. Our body language conveys our response. It's usually a one-to-one question. You don't want other people around when you are having that sort of conversation. It is also a very deep question. It goes to the core of our identity, because what we love, and who we love, defines the people we are.

As a Christian, I have been asked many times if I 'believe in Jesus', but only rarely have I been asked, 'Do you love Jesus?' In our culture, that would be to move into uncomfortable territory. That's getting too personal, even sentimental you might think. Fine to ask children such a question, but not an adult. I don't think my experience is uncommon in this regard. Christians may sing about loving Jesus. Most are more comfortable talking about belief in Jesus rather than loving him.

And yet it was with the question, 'Do you love me?' that Jesus challenged Peter, a close friend who had badly let him down. It was after Jesus' resurrection, in a one-to-one conversation. Peter clearly found it uncomfortable at the time because he was very conscious of his failure and deep sense of shame. So we need to look back to the last night of Jesus' life on earth, to Peter's failure, in order to understand the impact and significance of Jesus' question.

Failure and regrets

Peter's very public failure is recorded in all four Gospels.

He had failed to be the person he thought he was. On the

last night of his life on earth, Jesus had warned his friends that he was going to be arrested and killed. He also predicted that they would all run away in fear and desert him. But Peter insisted, 'Even if all fall away, I will not' (Mk 14:29). Peter had thought he was a cut above his mates and wasn't afraid to say it. He also boasted, 'Even if I have to die with you, I will never disown you' (Mk 14:31). But, when the authorities came to arrest Jesus, he had run away like all the others and left Jesus to face his enemies by himself. He failed to keep his promise.

Peter had failed Jesus in his time of greatest need. Later that evening, he did pluck up enough courage to creep into the back of the high priest's house where Jesus was being questioned and abused. One of the servants thought she recognised Peter as a friend of Jesus. Three times he denied that he even knew Jesus, the last time with swearing and oaths. 'I don't *xxxx* know that man!' he said – insert whatever expletives you like. Then the cock crowed, signifying that morning was coming, and Peter remembered that Jesus had warned him, 'Before the rooster crows twice, you yourself will disown me three times' (Mk 14:30), and Peter went outside, and broke down and wept. He learnt that he wasn't as strong as he thought he was. He also realised that Jesus knew him better than he knew himself.

After Jesus died, Peter must have been consumed with regret and remorse and a great sense of failure and shame. He had seen Jesus hanging on a cross and his body laid in the tomb. It seemed like it was too late to make amends, too late even to say 'sorry'.

Even after Jesus' resurrection, Peter's guilt and shame seems still to have been unresolved. He had seen the empty tomb. He had met Jesus, risen from the dead. When Jesus appeared to his disciples, it wasn't to blame them for their failure. He greeted them as friends: 'Peace be with you' (Jn 20:26). But still, Peter must have been asking himself: 'Can Jesus ever forgive *me* for what I did? Is there any place for *me* in Jesus plans? Have I blown it completely?'

I wonder if there are any of us who have not felt regret and experienced failure in some area of life at some point. We may fail to be the people we want to be in our marriage, as a parent or in holding to our standards. We may be a great success in our work and a failure at home, or the other way around. Very few of us can cover all the bases. We certainly all fail to be the loving, faithful, honest people God called us to be.

We may look back on some episodes in our life and wish we could press the rewind button and play it through again differently. There may be events in our past that we would like to erase from our memories. We might cringe at the thought of people knowing about our past failures. We may portray an image of ourselves so that people respect us and like us, but that image may be far from the reality.

That's why failure is usually a humbling and painful experience. Failure can bring shame on ourselves and our family. Failure may leave us feeling that we are of no value. Think of how you would feel if you knew that for the next 2,000 years, millions of people all around the world were going to be reading about you and your failures. We are still remembering Peter's failures here!

But failure can also be a great learning experience, as it was for Peter. It has a way of bringing us back from the fantasy land we sometimes like to live in, in order to face the truth about ourselves. It can show us what is really in our heart.

A personal encounter

It's against this backdrop of Peter's failure and sense of shame that Jesus has an in-depth conversation with him on the beach, on the shore of Lake Galilee.

Jesus took Simon Peter aside. He addressed him as 'Simon Son of John', the same name he used when he'd first called Peter to follow him three years before, and asked this question: 'Simon son of John, do you love me more than these?'

'Yes Lord, you know that I love you,' Peter replied. He no longer boasted that he loved Jesus *more* than anyone else. He simply affirmed that Jesus knew what was in his heart.

Jesus asked him again, 'Simon, son of John, do you love me?' Peter repeated his answer, 'Yes Lord, you know that I love you.'

Jesus asked him a third time, and that touched a raw nerve with Peter, no doubt because Peter had denied knowing Jesus three times. 'Peter was hurt because Jesus asked him the third time, "Do you love me?" He said, "'Lord, you know all things; you know that I love you'" (Jn 21:17). Why did Jesus ask that particular question, 'Do you love me?' Jesus didn't ask Peter about what was in the past. He didn't ask, 'Why did you do it, Peter? Why did you deny me? Why did you let me down so badly when I most needed some support from my friends?' He didn't remonstrate with him and say, 'Don't ever do that again!' He didn't try to get Peter to promise that he would do better in future. Instead, Jesus just focused on the present. He asked, 'Do you love me?' It was a 'now' question.

Forgiveness, reassurance and restoration

How could Peter live with himself after his humiliating failure? Peter, who became a great leader of the church, would be known forever as the one who had let Jesus down. He would have been aware of critics talking behind his back: 'Did you hear about the way he denied Jesus? I can't believe he's got the nerve to stand up and tell us what to believe and how to live!'

But Peter could live boldly as a follower of Jesus because he knew that Jesus had forgiven him. Peter learnt that Jesus knew the real person, not the image that Peter had wanted to portray. He knew Jesus loved him as he was.

In this encounter, Jesus did more than forgive Peter. He reassured him that he was forgiven. He restored Peter's relationship with him. He even strengthened that relationship, because it was now based on Peter's much deeper understanding of Jesus and a more realistic knowledge of himself.

When I was in my 20s and had just become a Christian, I became particularly conscious of all the shortcomings in my life and my repeated failing to live the life I thought God wanted me to live. It was then that someone asked me, 'What do you think God expects of you?'

I thought of possible answers. To serve him? To be a better person? But my questioner gave me this surprising response. 'God expects nothing of you but failure ... but he has given you his Holy Spirit that you need not fail.' He went on to say that God knows what we are like inside, and we can't pretend to him. In the penetrating words of Psalm 139, 'You know when I sit and when I rise; you perceive my thoughts from afar. You discern my going out and my lying down; you are familiar with all my ways' (vv. 1–2).

This may sound like a disturbing intrusion into our privacy, but it is deeply reassuring. It tells us that God knows all the weaknesses and the strengths of our character. He knows our personality. He made us. He knows even our best efforts to live a better life are likely to fail, but through Jesus, he forgives and restores failures. And he has given us his Holy Spirit that we need not keep on failing.

Jesus reassures us just as he reassured Peter: 'I know what you are like, I know what you've done – and I haven't given up on you.' He had a job for Peter to do – yes – Peter who had failed! (Jn 21:15–17). We learn here that Jesus does not discard failures. He restores us when we fail and entrusts us with work to do for him.

This is the amazing grace of God – forgiven, restored and entrusted by Jesus with a new role. It sets us free from worrying about what others think of us or what others know about our past. Like Peter, we can stop pretending to be what we are not and enjoy the freedom that comes from Jesus' acceptance of us as we are.

A personal response

We learn something wonderful about Jesus here. He is clearly more concerned with the attitude of our hearts, here and now, rather than what we have said or done in the past, good or bad.

Christian faith has an intellectual dimension. God has given us a mind to think with and to understand. It's also very practical, because true faith always shows itself in caring actions for other people. But at the centre is a love for Christ that springs from his love for us.

As we have seen, Jesus asked many questions in order to get us to to think, several others aimed at changing our attitudes and behaviour, but this question 'Do you love me?' goes straight to the heart, and calls for a response.

As with Peter, Jesus does not ask us the question, 'Have you messed up in the past?' He knows that we have! He simply asks, 'Do you love me?'

Further reading: John 21

www.ingramcontent.com/pod-product-compliance
Lightning Source LLC
LaVergne TN
LVHW051603080426
835510LV00020B/3113